PRAISE FOR
The Addict's Mom Presents
UNEXPECTED HEROES

"Heroes, indeed. Dedicated, devoted and drafted into a war that wasn't theirs, the parents of children suffering from addiction who are raising their grandchildren, also suffer—and too often, they suffer alone. Bravely exposing their hearts and lives, these heroes who share their stories in this book, bring understanding to the complex layers and devastating realities of the disease of addiction, while helping others hunkered down on the same battlefield to feel less isolated and alone. A beautiful composition of courage, compassion, wisdom, strength, love, honesty and hard truths, *Unexpected Heroes* is heartbreaking; but also enlightening and empowering. This book is a must-read for those on the front lines in the fight against addiction. No more shame, no more silence."

—Sandra Swenson,
author of *The Joey Song*

"Impressive and dedicated stories of parents who bravely accepted the challenge of raising their grandchildren due to the addictions of their own children and recognize the blessings. Not only will parents of addicts benefit from reading *Unexpected Heroes*, but also those who care to understand their journey. Lynne Gassel and Laura Chapman have truly been inspired and have produced a gifted work that will touch your heart."

—Karen Best Wright,
author of *I Love You From The Edges:
Lessons From Raising Grandchildren*

"*Unexpected Heroes* is an unflinching look at the ways in which addiction affects the entire family. The impact of an addicted parent on a child's life is cataclysmic. *Unexpected Heroes* shines a light on families who step up to rescue their grandchildren from the chaos, neglect and abuse caused by their addict children. The stories shared are real life accounts of families in crisis told by those who have weathered the storms and remain unbowed in their fight to save the children. This book offers a close look into the collateral effects of addiction as well as the ways in which grandparents learned to cope, survive and work towards healing the children in their care. The wisdom offered within these pages is a valuable resource for families who struggle with this issue, are fighting for the best interest of the children involved, and may feel they are alone in the battle."

—Deborah Doucette,
author of *Raising Our Children's Children:
Room in the Heart* and *The Forgotten Roses*

"There is a unique group of people who selflessly put their own lives, their time and their retirement on hold, day in and day out. They do this by working tirelessly to build, repair and save young lives—the lives of their grandchildren—who are the innocent victims and often "forgotten ones" left behind due to their parent's addiction. *Unexpected Heroes* gives the reader an honest glimpse into these mothers' lives. Without shame or resentment, they openly describe the trials and (more importantly) rewards of essentially becoming surrogate parents overnight. Very highly recommended reading not only for those who may be raising the offspring of their addicted children, but also for anyone who stands to be positively enlightened by the stories of these exceptional individuals."

—Judy Herzanek,
Changing Lives Foundation
co-author of *Why Don't They Just Quit*

"Addiction is a disease unlike any other—no one is immune. Parents and families are rendered helpless as they watch their loved ones spiral out of control; making risky decisions rarely in their best interest that often can prove fatal. In their inspiring new book; *Unexpected Heroes*, Lynne and Laura show us just how deep a grandparent's love can be and the sacrifices—no matter how painful—they're willing to make for their loved ones. *Unexpected Heroes* is a compilation of short stories by Lynne, Laura and other mothers who unexpectedly found themselves becoming parents of their grandchildren. This book shows how far families will go for the love of their children, how blindsided they really were and how fierce that love runs. *Unexpected Heroes* is one of those rare books you can't put down. A must read for anyone who has a child struggling with addiction. I also highly recommend this book to the families who think this could never happen to them and those who may mistakenly place blame on the parents of the addicts."

—Patricia Rosen,
publisher of *The Sober World Magazine*

"I recommend this book to anyone who has taken guardianship of a loved one's children due to drug addiction. The raw, gut-wrenching stories of those on the front lines of this fight will help you to understand you are not alone in the battle; and the wisdom that is spun into the tapestry of each story will give you the direction you need to keep your sanity in the midst of great pain and confusion."

—Mark Turansky,
author of *Figure it Face it & Fix it:*
Your Surprising Solution to Addictions and Substance Abuse

The Addict's Mom Presents
UNEXPECTED HEROES

The Addict's Mom Presents
UNEXPECTED HEROES

Stories of Love and Sacrifice in the Face of Addiction

LYNNE GASSEL
AND
LAURA CHAPMAN

TheAddictsMom.Org

Published By
TheAddictsMom.Org, Davie, Florida 33328

Printed By
CreateSpace, An Amazon.com Company

The names and identifying details of some characters and events in this book have
been changed.
The authors of this book are not accountable for the contents of the stories, if written
by others.

We dedicate this book to all the parents who have bravely chosen to fight on the front lines of the war against drugs and have become Unexpected Heroes in the eyes of their grandchildren. Your unselfish commitment to saving the smallest and most innocent victims of this war will never be forgotten. We pray that you will be blessed in ways you never could have imagined.

CONTENTS

FOREWORD

When I discovered two of my sons were using drugs, my life fell apart. For months I felt isolation, desperation and unbearable heartache. I couldn't function, I couldn't sleep, I couldn't work; all I did was focus on them. My family suffered, my friendships suffered, and I walked away from my own very successful business in order to dedicate myself to their recovery. Deep inside, I knew there were many other mothers suffering as I was. I wanted to create a place for all addict's moms to gather; a safe place where they would have the freedom to share their anguish without the burden of shame and guilt that comes with having an addicted child. Thus, The Addict's Mom with the mission of Sharing Without Shame was born, allowing broken spirits find healing, hope and comfort in the darkness of addiction.

When Lynne Gassel joined The Addict's Mom, she discovered that there were many grandparents who were raising their grandchildren due to addiction, just as she was. Lynne and other TAM grandparents consulted with me about the need for a specialized TAM group to support these grandparents. And so, The Addict's Mom G2G (Grandparent to Grandparent.) was created.

With Lynne Gassel as the facilitator, G2G has become a valuable resource.

I am very pleased to present our newest project: *Unexpected Heroes: Stories of Love and Sacrifice in The Face of Addiction* by G2G members and writers, Lynne Gassel and Laura Chapman. These remarkable women present a compelling view, as well as their own special insight into the challenges, angst and joys of raising grandchildren in the face of addiction. It is their wish to raise awareness not just of this issue, but to offer a glimpse into this very unexpected world where precious young lives are protected.

—Barbara Theodosiou
Founder, The Addict's Mom

ACKNOWLEDGEMENTS

Our deepest appreciation to The Addict's Mom Non-Profit Organization and especially to founder, Barbara Theodosiou, for supporting us in the publishing of this book.

To our husbands, Stu and Rich, we thank them forever, for their love and support.

We are grateful beyond words to the following "Unexpected Heroes" who, along with us, have volunteered to share their stories without shame: Teresa Adams, Patti Aguirre, Cheri May Blackburn, Joy Bury, C. Deane Campbell, Sandee Barton, Pattee Russell-Curry, Candace Dufresne, Mari Elena, Betty Hanway, Denise Hoff, Julie Corbin-Hulsey, Jerri R. Jackson, Jennifer Meadows, Janice Johnson, Lauren Leigh Cordiner, Susan B. McArdle, Cathy McElhaney, Karen O'Hara, Kathy Petrin, Jackie Riddle, Kami Turner, Renea Weber, Bonnie Worth and Elaine Nicholas, Compassion Fatigue Educator, for kindly contributing her expertise.

This book would not have been possible without your unwavering courage, generosity and commitment.

ACKNOWLEDGMENTS

INTRODUCTION

"We didn't set out to be superheroes. But
sometimes, life doesn't go the way you planned."

—*Big Hero 6, 2015*

We felt alone, isolated and embarrassed. No one could possibly understand what we were experiencing. Many of us tried to mask our dual lives with smiles and excuses, hoping the situation was only temporary. We wondered what we had done wrong to have an addicted child and how in the world we ended up raising their children.

Subsequently, either by searching for answers or just blind luck, we discovered a website, The Addict's Mom G2G (Grandparent to Grandparent). Suddenly, our loneliness began to fade. We found others who could relate to the uncharted territory we faced at a place in our lives when we had much different plans.

We felt their pain, related to their stories and immediately recognized ourselves. We were all raising our children's children, the innocent victims caught in the crossfire of the war against drugs and not one of us stood idly by. Without giving it a second thought, we had stepped in to do whatever we could to save them, even if it meant permanently entering into the parenting arena again.

Yet, there was no model, no precedent on how to be a parent to our grandchildren. Aging bodies and minds challenged some of us. Many of us were single or widowed and on limited incomes. Several of us were retired and many of us were unable to retire and continued to work a full-time job. We had been drafted to fight a war we didn't choose but we readily accepted it. We couldn't possibly appreciate the stress and magnitude of potential problems ahead, along with the identity crisis we were about to experience. Nor did we realize we were members of a much larger growing family. Surprisingly, seven million children across the country live in households headed by grandparents, according to the *2014 Census Bureau Report*. This number may be significantly larger because so much of the information goes unreported.

These are our stories. Our grandchildren came to us from a myriad of different scenarios. They had birth parents that were in active addiction or early recovery, were incarcerated, suffered untreated mental illness or unfortunately and too often, lost the fight with their dependence on drugs and forfeited their lives.

Most of our grandchildren appeared to be well-adjusted, healthy kids. Unfortunately, many of them were dealing with the challenges of abandonment, physical and/or emotional abuse or learning disabilities. From both nature (drug use during pregnancy) and nurture (drug use during the child's life), many of these children had not received the proper love, security or care they deserved when they came to us.

The stories that follow illustrate how we, as grandparents, decided to confront these obstacles and take on this new Grandparent/ Parent role with dedication, determination and love. We chose to fight for our grandchildren to save them from the chains of their parent's addiction and give them a nurturing, safe and stable home. As a result, we became "Unexpected Heroes" in the eyes of the children we saved. But most of us found that we received much more than we gave.

I

THE BATTLE BEGINS

"We do not have to become heroes overnight.
Just a step at a time, meeting
each thing that comes up
discovering we have the strength to stare it down."

—*ELEANOR ROOSEVELT*

THE BEGINNING OF
THE APOCALYPSE

LarLei's Story

My precious son, your addiction saga began thirteen years and fifty-eight days after your birth. I received a phone call from the ER telling me nurses were pumping your stomach of ibuprofen, cold tablets and cough syrup, while your lungs were fighting to expel the Butane you had huffed. I learned the little girl from across the street had played the same dangerous game with you. She was in the cubicle next to yours. On the emergency room bed, your body was lax, eyelids were heavy and your dad's girlfriend was holding your hand. The tube had been removed from your throat but the bottle on the wall still held the red remains of your stomach. I thought it was strawberries.

"No," the girlfriend said. "Cherry Nyquil."

Your father arrived, still dressed in his cop's duty uniform and stood in your room without sitting all night—waiting for lab results, the Baker Act to legally declare you mentally incompetent so we could have you evaluated and his embarrassment when everyone would find out.

The behavioral center driver arrived and he loaded you and the little girl from across the street along with some other big guy into an unmarked police car. I followed right behind. At four thirty in the morning, after more why-did-you-do-its, the behavioral center's evaluator said you could not be released to your parents until seen by the psychiatrist, who would begin rounds at six, starting with the children.

I drove home exhausted and managed to sleep between the mattress and a fitful dream for an hour until your father called. "The psychiatrist telephoned in a diagnosis of Attention Deficit Disorder," he reported. He's prescribing Ritalin."

I said, "Over my dead body!"

Your father simply responded, "Okay." Apparently he thought this was an argument.

"We'll talk about it later," I stated. "But I am not putting more chemicals in my child's body without another opinion."

Before I could bulldoze the behavioral center walls to get to you, the spry little social worker sat me down with the good doctor's diagnosis. "Attention Deficit Hyperactivity Disorder," she announced. "Impulsive, doesn't consider the consequences, tosses and turns at night—doesn't that sound like him?" she asked.

So that's the reason, I thought, why you, at thirteen years old, swallowed seventeen Ibuprofen, four Alka-Seltzer cold tablets, three-fourths of a bottle of Cherry Nyquil and huffed Butane?

I was sure it was much more complicated than that. And yet, the man whose name ended with PhD made this "accurate" diagnosis by asking you complicated questions, without your parents present, at six o'clock in the morning, after you'd been through a night of abusing over-the-counter-drugs, huffed a dangerous gas, had your stomach pumped and laid for six hours on a hospital bed with the lights on?

"Here is a prescription for Ritalin. Don't give it to him before bedtime or in the summer," he said.

"Aren't there side effects?"

"It's a low dose and kids have gone from making D's and F's in school to B's and A's in just a few days. Here's some information from *America Online*."

"Thanks." Hesitantly, I took the paper. Eleven cyber-pages to support the good doctor's diagnosis and glorify Ritalin. Should I really give you this prescription, I thought, starting this morning, in place of food for your body or love for your soul without even attempting to address what the real issue might be?

On the way out, we stopped at the processor's desk. She instructed: "Sign on the line, please." We walked through the double doors. I held my breath. You were calm but you were not okay. We slid into the car for the ride back home.

I felt uncertain, my head racked with worry. I was positive that we had been simply dealt with and then brushed aside. I knew there had to be other answers; other questions that I wasn't even sure how to ask. Thinking this was going to be a wild ride, I said, "Buckle your seat belt." I couldn't even begin to imagine how right I would be.

NOBODY ASKED

Not one of us ever planned for our children to grow up to be addicts. After all, we gave them good lives. Did we give them too much? Did we not give them enough? With so many questions, we began our search for answers, and discovered there really weren't any. And that was, perhaps, the hardest answer of all to accept.

Laura's Story

When I was contemplating the "white picket fence" years ago, I really thought I had it all. I did my homework, studied hard, said "I do" to the right man, packed up all the right stuff and set off to conquer the world.

I was optimistic and excited.

Along the way I kept a regular running conversation with God and knew without a doubt that He approved of my efforts.

Over thirty years later, I know that the picket fence is an illusion. I can't study hard enough. I still love the same man with all my heart and there are many days when the world swiftly and thoroughly conquers me.

But I continue to talk to God and I know, even now, he approves of my efforts—and that's enough.

I'm still optimistic.

Having said that, I never asked to be living in a fire.

Never even dreamed that a monster could come into my home and steal one of my children.

Never imagined I'd be held in the grip of fear every day wondering where she was, what she was doing, if she was eating, sleeping or safe.

I never asked for a daily struggle to simply complete ordinary tasks and stay focused on being productive so the minimum that must be completed each day gets done. And too often it doesn't.

I never asked to be vulnerable to things that I couldn't have dreamed would touch my life.

I never asked to be truly afraid, even terrified of the events each new day might bring.

I never asked to cry so much.

I never asked for a child addicted to drugs.

BLIND-SIDED

For most of us, our reaction the first time we were faced with the realization our children were abusing drugs was one of absolute shock. This kind of thing was what happened to "other" people. Not us. Many of our children came from great homes in good neighborhoods with attentive, loving parents.

Lynne's Story

It's easy to fool ourselves into thinking we have our lives perfectly planned out. It was that way for me as a product of the 1950s and '60s. I'd go to college, meet my prince, get married, have children and, of course, live happily ever after. As much as I was sure I knew what to expect, my life was blind-sided. This turned the world, as I knew it, upside down.

My husband and I were thoroughly exhausted. Still in shock, we had finally accepted the undeniable fact our daughter was using drugs and had just made the three-hour road trip to her college to give her an ultimatum—either come home for treatment or lose our support. At first, she laughed when we asked her to take the drug test. Then, to our relief, she reluctantly chose to come home while she continued to argue why the drug test we gave her *had* to be wrong. She had tested positive for cocaine. We gathered up all her belongings, threw them in her suitcases and drove another stressful three hours on tenterhooks hoping she wouldn't jump out of the car at the next red light.

We arrived home by midnight but neither of us slept well worried our daughter would slip away in the night. My husband and I held onto each other tightly, hoping it would help us fall asleep, but we couldn't sleep. I kept listening for footsteps going down the stairs, the front door to open or the start of a car engine. Thankfully, the night was uneventful.

In the morning, we drove straight to the outpatient rehab facility located inside our local hospital. The rehab counselor we spoke to before picking up our daughter advised us a nine-month outpatient rehab had a higher success rate with younger adults because they attended the daily program for a longer period of time. I hoped he was correct.

As we quietly rode the empty elevator, I felt like I was having an out-of-body experience when we stopped at the floor labeled "Chemical Dependency Treatment." I never imagined anyone from our family would be here and desperately hoped I wouldn't see anyone I knew. I didn't want to have to explain anything, at least not yet. After following a few winding corridors, we reached the front desk. The receptionist was very friendly and asked if we'd like water or coffee while we waited.

I'd rather have a new life.

How could this be our life? My husband and I didn't smoke or do drugs. If we had a random glass of wine, it was a big deal. When our kids were teens, I can remember doing the typical safety checks like smelling their breath for traces of alcohol and discreetly checking the pupils of their eyes for drug use. I was always relieved when nothing was detected.

We were living a traditional upper middle class life with four kids who were social, bright, active and educated. The two eldest were college graduates, one getting an advanced degree, and the two youngest were in college. This didn't happen to people like us, did it?

Too soon we would learn addiction is not particular about its victims. It's a crapshoot.

Our daughter, who from a young age lacked self-esteem and allowed boys to define her, began her drug use by smoking marijuana with her first boyfriend and graduated to cocaine with her second. But nine months of outpatient rehab still didn't stop her and cocaine remained her drug of choice until the fateful night she tried methamphetamine. She was at a party, couldn't score any cocaine and was offered meth. Scared to death, she tried it anyway and loved it. Immediately addicted, there was no turning back and within five tumultuous years, she spiraled down, ended up on the street and became pregnant.

The day she called us with the news, I was glad I was sitting down. Proud and excited by her accomplishments, she told me not to speak but to just listen. She proceeded to tell me how she had stopped using as soon as she discovered she was pregnant, had acquired state-funded insurance, food stamps, was living with the grandmother of her friend and the father was not involved. My husband and I thought perhaps this was her turnaround. She had taken on responsibility without our help and seemed to be headed in the right direction.

After a couple months, the grandmother, at whose house she was staying, called me to say she thought our daughter would do better living with us and was also feeling a bit cramped with the extra houseguest. When it was clear to us she was clean, we brought her home and life seemed almost normal. My daughter was less stressed and life and laughter seemed to return to what it was before drugs. Giving birth to a child and being drug-free for most of the pregnancy, we hoped her sobriety would stick—and it did, for a while. But before her beautiful baby boy was two years old, her demons were back full-force and we had to make the gut-wrenching decision to ask her to leave our home to get sober. Rather than go into a locked-down facility where we knew she'd have the best chance at sobriety, she chose to enter a sober-living home. Meanwhile, we promised to temporarily care for the baby and trusted she'd return to him soon.

Unfortunately, during her six-month stay, she was hardly sober, finally got caught using and was immediately kicked out. She went from one friend's sofa to another and three years later, was arrested for possession of drugs and identity theft. After five torturous months in jail, she finished her one-year sentence in a court-ordered rehab. But by then it was too late. Tragically, our daughter died in a hospital emergency room, all alone, from a pulmonary emboli most likely caused by her ten years of drug use.

Again, we were in shock. We had not only just lost a daughter but we also became unexpected real parents to our grandson. What we thought would be temporary became permanent.

Called Mommy and Daddy since our precious grandson was three years old, he hardly saw or remembered his birth mom and referred to her by her first name since calling us Mom and Dad. I would share good memories of her and tell him she was his "belly" mom and I was his "heart" mom. The birth father remained absent, which made everything less complicated for us.

However, this child was the product of two addicts, giving us cautionary pause. Of course, we didn't know if he carried an addictive gene but with his chances being so high, we felt an increased responsibility to prepare him in case of future challenges. We also saw a need for him to have play therapy to work out any issues that would most likely arise. His therapist counseled us to be forthright about his history. Knowing that, we were honest about his birth parents' struggles and explained everything to him in an age-appropriate manner around the age of four.

He just turned eleven and we've been teaching him to make good choices, along with educating him about addiction. Yet, as wonderful and prepared as he seems to be, will he make the right choices when he's a hormonal teenage kid who trusts his peers and thinks he's omnipotent? Ultimately, it will be up to him. With every breath, we hope and pray that he will.

SHELL-SHOCKED

It's surprising to note that, more often than not, children who use drugs are typically far above average in intelligence, talent and potential. A 2010 study that ran in *Psychology Today* stated that those with an IQ of 125 or higher are exponentially more likely to use drugs. Knowing this and having such high hopes for our clearly gifted children only made the realization worse. How could this have happened to our family? Surely, it must have been a mistake. But it wasn't.

C. Deane's Story

I always thought of my daughter as special. She was beautiful, intelligent, a leader. People had always been drawn to her. She had boyfriends in elementary school and teachers found her to be mature for her years. We had our boy first and then a girl—the "Perfect American Family." We were also working class parents, facing the proposition of raising a family on a fairly low income.

When my daughter was born and I was joyfully counting her fingers and toes, I held her close and whispered, "My sweet baby, you will go through this one day. But only after college where you will meet an educated man and together have the means to provide the best for your children. This is the good life. I want this for you." That memory has resurfaced many times.

Life flew past in a whirl of T-ball and soccer, dance and Girl Scouts, church and sports. My daughter was musically talented and played the flute. As a dancer, she had a passion for performing and loved that we participated together. I was the dance studio emcee during those performances and delighted in sewing her costumes and watching her dance.

She also excelled in sports and we saw the same parents and kids at every sport and event. At the time, I perceived us to be the "cream of the crop." Our kids were the "good kids" and I doubt there was a parent in that group who didn't feel pride at all of our children's accomplishments. After all, good parents created good kids. I think many of us believed that. I know I did.

It was a teammate on one of those sports teams who opened the door to Hell. This little girl was sweet and truly believed she was helping my daughter find a solution to her problem. My daughter was in seventh grade and like all the women in our family, very much taller than most girls her age. She was not large—just bigger, and had started to mature. But she saw herself as fat when compared to her prepubescent friends with bodies shaped like skinny hot dogs. She told me later she complained to her friend on the recreation basketball team about being fat. That friend had an older fifteen-year-old sister who was drop-dead gorgeous and who maintained her figure by smoking "this stuff." The friend introduced our daughter to her sister and at age thirteen, our dear naïve innocent child tried methamphetamine. Her memory was it scared her. "Mom, I knew I'd never be able to not smoke it again. I knew it the very first time."

My daughter's body image issues continued as she refused to dress down for physical education and failed that class every year thereafter. Oh boy, I thought, teenage rebellion. But today, I now realize I was watching burgeoning addiction, which often mimics many other stages of growth. I should have known better. I knew the warning signs—changed attitude, changed looks or dress and changing friends. But when I presented my concerns to our family doctor, she noted that all of her teens went through the same thing and by graduation, most returned to where they were before. I was relieved. Even so, my A-student, class leader began failing more classes. As the year progressed, she failed English and math for non-participation. I remained in denial.

Then in eighth grade, there was a locker search and a note was discovered in my daughter's locker. It was addressed to a boy her age suspected by the school staff of dealing drugs. The note from my daughter appeared to be seeking some sort of drug. I attended the requested meetings with staff and nodded appropriately at their concern, but they didn't know her like I did. My kid would not seek out drugs. Furthermore, I had met the boy and he was a cutie. She probably just wanted to get close to him. So we grounded her from television for a night and banned any future contact with the boy who was later expelled from school on drug charges.

This behavior that had developed in middle school did not abate when she entered high school. The school automated call system was regularly calling our home to report missed classes. But my daughter was charming and intelligent. She would tell me that a teacher was unfair or didn't like her or punished her for someone else's misdeeds. She told me her excuse for missing class was either her teacher was distracted during attendance or another teacher refused to mark her present when she was just ten minutes late. She was so believable. And I wanted to believe her. I wanted her to return to the good kid that I remembered. I wanted to still be the good parent.

Her vice principal called me for a meeting with a teacher who planned to fail my daughter for non-participation. The teacher was furious, which made me furious. She accused my daughter of being high in class. My daughter, of course, denied the accusation and dumped out her backpack when she was asked to prove she wasn't carrying drugs. I can remember feeling vindicated when no evidence was found. After all, hadn't my daughter said the teachers were picking on her? I resolved to not doubt her again. But the trouble continued and at the end of the term, she was expelled for skipping class and being disruptive.

About that time, I got a phone call. Three of my daughter's friends were on the call and they wanted me to know she was smoking meth. I was standing when I got the call and actually fell to the ground in shock. My husband thought I was having a heart attack. I couldn't breathe. I couldn't think. Some part of me absolutely believed those girls. But when my daughter came home, she explained she had started seeing one of the girl's boyfriends and they had done this to get back at her. Indeed, two weeks later, one of the girls recanted the story. I was relieved. Again.

It was Monday and I was at work when I received a call from her. She had spent the night with a friend whom I knew and liked. She said to me, "Destiny's mom said I had to call. I didn't spend the night at her house. I was out all night with other friends. I showed up at Destiny's house in the morning and wanted them to lie for me. She said either I call you, or she would." Suddenly, all the pieces were clicking in my brain. A sixteen-year-old had no reason to be out all night unless it was drug-related. So I picked her up and on the way home, I told her we were stopping by the doctor's office for a urine analysis. To my surprise, she agreed.

The doctor called me himself. The test came back positive for meth. I was crying uncontrollably and asked him, "Who do we call? Where can I take her to get this fixed?" He offered to pray with me on the phone. But my "perfect parent" went into hyperdrive. I spent the next thirty-six hours surfing the Internet for information and solutions.

It was grim. There were few youth facilities available, none that specialized in meth addiction and none would post cure rates or even success rates. Finally, after being up all night, I called a center about one hundred and fifty miles from our home. The lady who answered had an addict son and told me how to convince my daughter to come in for an evaluation. I even wrote down a script to convince her to come with me to a fairly distant city. To my utter shock, it worked.

I drove her there in a snowstorm that turned into a blizzard. The usual three-hour drive took eleven hours. I gripped the wheel with both hands and refused to stop for fear I would never get her back in the car. But we made it. The facility seemed like a good one with a strong family program. While my child went through two days of orientation and testing, parents were required to attend a two-day education session.

I immediately hit it off with one of the dads whose daughter reminded me very much of my own. However, at the end of the two days, I thought it peculiar that he and I were called into meetings separate from the other parents. The news they had to deliver nearly knocked me to my knees, again. They were refusing to keep my daughter for treatment because she posed too great of a flight risk. She and the other girl had both been adamant that if they were left at the center, they would run away. Once again, this perfect parent was speechless with anxiety.

The counselor brought my daughter in and told her the news, which appeared to make her very happy. But with skill and empathy, the counselor went on to convince my daughter to enter outpatient treatment and to return for residential treatment at the first positive urinalysis test (UA) result. At that point, she would have agreed to sell her skin just to go home. It took another two months of raging and bad behavior before the outpatient clinic reported a dirty UA result, and another month to get a bed. But she was true to her word and went back into inpatient treatment.

Anyone with an addict child will tell you that when a child attends treatment, the relief felt is almost euphoric. For the first time in three years, I slept at night. I attended all the family sessions, visited every weekend, purchased new clothes for my daughter, rebonded with her as a sober young adult and sent her post cards and letters almost every day. I wanted her to feel like she had won the lottery. And part of me wanted to be sure she felt guilty enough to stay, no matter how difficult she perceived it to be. But she enjoyed the stay.

The kids were kids like her, from good families with good insurance. Indeed, I found I bonded with the other parents as much as my daughter bonded with her group mates. But then we hit the three-week mark and along with my excitement, anxiety began to return. She was coming home. For the first time in years, we thought we might get back the "perfect" kid we lost three years before. She had a lot to make up—missed school, job applications and driving lessons. I remember thinking she just needed to get back on track (as though her addiction had been something like a broken leg that kept her from skiing).

That summer, on her return, she signed up for a college class in English that could make up for all the failed English classes to date. She excelled, as I knew she would and received an A. My kid, who basically had not attended school since sixth grade, passed a college level English course with flying colors. Ha! Maybe that would show them she was a good kid and she was bright as well as beautiful. This would prove to them I knew my girl better than they.

It didn't last. Within two months, she was obviously using again. She returned for another forty days at rehab, this time followed by a three-month stay in a recovery house in another city. It was harder this time, as we all suddenly recognized treatment was not the "silver lining" we had perceived it to be. And my daughter's attitude was wretched. She lashed out at counselors, staff and family. It was a miserable time. But I continued with the cards, letters, gifts of clothing and phone cards. She relapsed on a home visit and at the end of her second month at the recovery house was told to leave.

When she came home she wouldn't follow our house rules. I also noticed a sudden drop in her weight—a sure sign she had returned to meth. We kicked her out. Home is where a kid is supposed to feel safe and we kicked her out.

Other parents, who did not have children with addiction issues, were more than willing to give us advice on how to "fix" our kid, and we were eager to listen. I figured to get the kid like the one they had, I should be a parent like they were. So I became a chameleon trying everything they suggested. We tried tough love and locked her out and then let her back in and then tried to forbid her from leaving the house. We took her phone and then returned it so we could track her down. We searched her belongings and violated her privacy on a regular basis. She went to another treatment center, which lasted four days. Then she was arrested for shoplifting and the court sent her to treatment at a run-down facility without a family program. And she loved it there.

But this time she surprised us. She graduated and also brought home a gift—a boy she had fallen in love with at rehab. Despite our best efforts they were married less than a year later. The boy was sweet. He was kind, loving and generous to a fault. And he also appeared to suffer from some sort of cognitive/maturity disorder. I didn't know his diagnosis, but there was something—a sort of permanent immaturity—that kept him from holding a job or understanding how to pay bills. He was continually seeking attention and associating with those who would accept him as he was. And those folks were mostly involved in the drug world.

As a couple they stayed sober long enough to have two babies fourteen months apart. But it was rough. There were fights and arguing and any time my daughter felt unsafe, she would call the police. Her husband was arrested four times in three months for domestic assault. But his mental condition was such that despite the constant arrests, he could not change his behavior nor keep his court appointments. After a year, the local judge sent him to prison because the four domestic violence charges were equivalent to a felony.

When my daughter's husband went to prison, she told me she not only feared being alone but also feared being responsible for others. So she slipped back into the easy acceptance of the drug world for company and back into our home for security.

One night our daughter wanted to go to a party but we refused to watch the babies. We thought forcing her to "be a mom" would somehow prevent her from returning to addiction. But she went anyway and took the babies with her. In the early morning hours, we got a call from one of her friends. Our daughter, our bright and kind daughter who had wanted to be the best mom ever, had left the party with a man. She had abandoned both children there.

I cannot remember being more horrified. I was so certain endangering her children was a line she would never cross. Not my daughter, not my kid. She wasn't like the other meth addicts. I was so sick in my codependence I had difficulty recognizing the truth even when it was right in front of me.

Circumstances deteriorated rapidly and our daughter ultimately ended up in jail. We took both boys, age three months and eighteen months, and it soon became obvious we needed to legalize our arrangement; so we filed for custody. Both parents signed.

After our daughter's release from jail, she moved into a group home. I made every effort to take the boys to visit her. We would meet at a park and she would try to play with them. But they had been with us for two years and by then, didn't recognize her as their mother. They responded to her as if she were a stranger.

During the last visit with her I noticed there was definitely something wrong. Her mental health had deteriorated to the point she was hearing voices and seeing things that weren't there. She yelled at the boys, which was a first and altogether out of character for her.

An assessment at the nearest hospital psychiatric ward confirmed she suffered from meth-induced psychosis. But she refused to be admitted so I brought her back home. Even with two years of being sober, the psychosis had worsened so much I was forced to have her arrested out of fear for our safety. In her deteriorated mental state, she ended up in jail, off and on, for assault and shoplifting. In jail, her insanity was uncontrollable. Upon release, she was incoherent, wandered the streets, stopped sleeping, eating and was committed to a mental health facility.

After so many years, to say we were shell-shocked is to say the least. We tried as much as possible to make the most of each day while still living in the shadow of our daughter's residual mental health issues caused by her addiction.

The boys are now seven and eight and continue to see their mom weekly. They know mommy is sick and her sickness came from drug use. They understand the "allergy to drugs and alcohol" runs in our family. They know drugs feel good and many kids use drugs, but they cannot because of the allergy.

Like my daughter, these boys are also special and exhibit many of the natural talents their mother had before drugs and mental illness took them away. The difference in raising them is we are no longer blind. We are trying to teach them respect for their bodies and how to make good choices, even at their young age. We are far more knowledgeable now of potential challenges they may face in the future, than the young parents we once were. I pray we know enough and have done everything we possibly can to help them make the right decisions.

CARE PACKAGES MISSING

Families of addicts often feel alone, unsupported and unable to reach out to others who can understand what they face. Raising awareness about the stigma of addiction and the challenges faced by these families is critical in order to fully support and offer them hope.

Laura's Story

I remember when I was a child and a family we knew was devastated when their son was in a head on collision. Fortunately, he survived but not without weeks of medical support that led to months of recovery. My mother responded immediately, along with the rest of the neighbors by making a casserole to take to them so they wouldn't have to worry about cooking. She also put together a care package of small items meant to lift the spirits of her friend, who was spending long hours at the hospital and then at home tending to the needs of her convalescing son.

Many years later that memory resurfaced when my daughter was born and almost immediately hospitalized again with a serious infection. Suddenly, we were the recipients of the kindness of others who brought food for several days for my family. I remember how awesome that food tasted—how truly touched I was to be embraced and supported by such kindness and concern with meals and sweet care packages of small gifts. When I received the phone call that revealed our daughter was using meth, I might as well have been in a head on collision. Ironically, this was the same child that made us the recipients of so many kindness casseroles and care packages when she was an infant. But this time there were no casseroles. There were no care packages.

Someone once said, "Addict's moms don't get casseroles," and the truth in that statement goes far beyond the words. The revelation our daughter was a drug addict immediately destroyed the stability and peace in our lives. But we couldn't even begin to know the true extent of the damage that had been done to our family that day as we began the fight for our daughter's life.

Addiction, we discovered, was an insidious evil that slowly worked its way into the smallest nooks and crannies of our lives until they became filled with darkness and fear. And we, like most families tried our best to pretend everything was fine and continue on as normally as possible until we simply couldn't any more.

Even in the face of the questions from well meaning friends, we held on to the idea we were simply facing a storm that would eventually pass. No need to make a big deal out of it, right? Everything would be ok. Our daughter was simply going through a phase she would eventually outgrow. Besides, addiction was certainly nothing we ever considered our family could possibly face and it was, quite honestly, embarrassing to have to admit it.

It didn't take very long, however, before we realized there was no quick fix to what we were facing. Once we were able to get beyond our initial paralysis, learning to live with an addicted child became a process and a learning experience. Each member of our family dealt with this differently and each was impacted to varying degrees. Keeping up a façade was impossible. So we got over whatever embarrassment we had felt and decided the truth was much easier. As we reached out to and gained knowledge of other families with similar stories, we came to understand we had nothing of which to be ashamed and that absolutely no family was immune.

Like every addict's family, we found the road ahead to be long and difficult. We clung to the stories of hope of those who were able to forever leave their addicted days behind. But we knew the reality of addiction was it could become a life long battle with multiple relapses. So many families live in the shadow of addiction; it could be considered the greatest epidemic.

This knowledge we were not alone didn't make the reality we faced any easier. Having an addicted loved one had changed us. We learned a new understanding of "one day at a time" and a new appreciation for small blessings previously taken for granted. Personally, very little in the way of challenges that come my way can faze me. I've stared straight into the eyes of the monsters that really do live in the closet and didn't back down saying, "I am a drug addict's mom, you can't scare me!"

I treasure the sober path my daughter now walks and pray for her daily she can remain steady and not fall. I never look down at other parents who may be facing behavior issues with their children and readily offer my support and guidance should those issues even appear to be leaning towards addiction. I know their pain too well and would gladly spend the rest of my life in an effort to help prevent other families from facing what we have faced. And I don't even like casseroles anymore for some reason, and that's really just fine.

HOLIDAY LEAVE DENIED

A lost sense of normalcy is what we long for but rarely seems to be part of our lives when addiction is present. Our families become so disjointed that even our traditions suffer.

Laura's Story

Where are you Christmas? We didn't even try to dig the Christmas decorations out of the closet under the stairs that year until half way through December. It was probably the first time our family tradition of decorating the day after Thanksgiving was abandoned. Instead of retiring to the family room in a turkey coma that day to relax and watch reruns of *Miracle on 42nd Street* or *I Wonderful Life*, leftovers were immediately packaged the moment we got up from the table to deliver to our homeless addict daughter. The reality of the necessity of that task completely sapped our holiday spirit and holiday decorating the next day was abandoned.

And then it just never returned. Somehow it was just too hard to focus on tinsel and lights, shopping and baking. The eight-foot, four-piece, pre-lit tree that took hours to assemble and decorate stayed in the boxes under the stairs. Instead, we set up the tiny two-foot tall blue tree on the chest near the front window and placed our gifts around it. It was the one with the angel on top that usually sat on a small table in the entryway. It seemed appropriate. At least it had one strand of blinking lights, which was about the size of our Christmas spirit, anyway. I actually felt good about making that much effort. I tried to remember what it felt like for my family to be whole. I missed the feeling when everyone I loved was all together and safe. I wondered if I would ever feel it again.

That year was always remembered as the year we lost Christmas. It was a year when we lost many things. Some of them were found again but others never were. Like so much stolen from us due to addiction, we came to realize the intangible things, like priceless memories of precious family time, were what we missed the most.

A WAR WE DIDN'T CAUSE

Dealing with the impact of addiction is a full-time job for parents of addicts. Our minds are never at rest. We conjure up every negative action from our past; questioning our attitudes, behaviors, our parenting skills—even our marriages and divorces. We try to make sense out of our child's addiction somehow by trying to assign a reason as to why it happened. And whom do we blame? Ourselves. These thoughts can literally consume us. Trying to understand what is truly incomprehensible can wreak as much havoc in our minds as in our lives. Yet, is there ever a rhyme or reason?

Cathy's Story

Sitting at the local diner, eating my breakfast, I couldn't help but overhear the conversation at the next table. The front page of the local newspaper that day had the pictures and a story of seven area young people who were arrested in a meth bust. The overheard comments were very predictable.

"Where were the parents?" one of them asked.

"That's what I want to know," another chimed in.

"Yes, it all begins in the home," someone else smugly declared. "That's why I always kept mine right at home."

Blah. Blah. Blah. Whatever, I thought. Clean off your own front porch before you try sweeping off mine.

Let me tell you the true stories of four friends all from the same small town. As you read these stories, you will see there is no rhyme or reason as to the manner addiction strikes one family or another. Call it fate, chance or bad luck. Is it anyone's fault? I don't think so.

My friend, Jackie, made her money questionably at the local bar. She used to tease me I worked too hard. She told me all I had to do was go to the bar and flirt a little. I could have a man for the weekend and on Sunday he would be gone. But my cupboards would be full, steaks would be on the grill and there would be one hundred dollars under my lamp.

Jackie had a total of six kids. Her only son was a truck driver with a very nice wife and family. One daughter was a pediatric nurse, a second daughter was married to a preacher, another worked at the local nursing home and a fourth was a student at Duke University. They all did well, except for one daughter, who struggled to stay sober and was one of the young people in the newspaper story busted for meth. One might try to link Jackie somehow to that daughter, but what about the rest of her kids?

Joanie was always a fighter. This started way back in third grade when she would fight girls, boys—anyone. She was one tough little girl. She grew up to be an over-the-road trucker and developed a drug habit. While on the road, she left her kids with anyone who would watch them. Sometimes she just left them, sadly, to fend for each other. She had all kinds of men, frequently partied and the police were often at her place. So often in fact, we used to wonder if anything was ever going to be done for those poor kids. They didn't seem to stand a chance. Yet, not one of them got into trouble. Her oldest became a forklift driver, another was a successful drummer in a regional band and her youngest was the night shift supervisor at a factory.

Jenny, my husband's sister, always worked hard and took good care of her three kids. She had married a policeman and her kids were always in the public eye, raising money for different charities. They were great kids, made honor roll every year and always had summer jobs. We had lots of fun together at family cookouts and camping.

Her oldest son, a diabetic, was on disability but had a nice family, lived near his mom and was doing great. Her youngest son was a college graduate with a good career. But her middle daughter became a heroin addict. She left home and was sleeping in rat-infested abandoned houses in a nearby city. She had four children. But the tragic death of one of them turned her life around and she decided to get sober and stayed sober. Then equally tragic, one of her children, Jenny's youngest granddaughter, became an addict. She was also mentioned in the front-page newspaper story.

As for me, all three of my girls were in 4-H Club, exhibiting at the county and state levels. My middle girl remains my bright spot. I tell her every day how much I love her and appreciate her. She is my best friend. My kids were all involved in community plays, band, show choir, art, church and family events. So it was quite a surprise when my oldest started using cocaine and prescription drugs at age seventeen. She is still addicted, today, at age thirty-nine. She is so damaged by the effects of drugs, accidents and beatings; it breaks my heart. I have custody of her son. He has been with me off and on since he was born and eventually, I received permanent guardianship of him. Even sadder, my oldest took four of her cousins and her youngest sister down that shadowy road to addiction with her. Tragically, my youngest—my baby who was so full of life, funny, smart, a married mother of two—died from a drug overdose. I didn't have the slightest clue she was using.

My mom, who was a hospice patient, had just moved in with us so I could care for her. She had been prescribed opiate medication and I was scared my oldest or one of the cousins would find them. I had no idea my youngest was the one who had started using. I was focused on my oldest daughter and my mom. I hid the drugs and only shared the information with the hospice nurse, my husband, middle daughter and unfortunately, my youngest daughter. One night she came to visit and unknown to any of us, stole my mother's morphine.

Later that night, my phone rang with a message I'll never forget. I could hardly process the info. What? What? Who died? My husband came in asking what was going on. That's when and how we learned of our youngest daughter's overdose. We both hit the floor crying and screaming until it seemed we couldn't breathe. To say it was painful was not even close. To add to this horrific night, my mom passed away twenty-three minutes after that phone call.

So whose fault was this? Who caused it? The stories of the young people mentioned in the newspaper, as well as others; and finally even in my own family clearly show there isn't a good answer. Where addiction should seem to happen—it didn't, and where it shouldn't—it did. Unfairly, there are plenty of ignorant people who know nothing about addiction and they are more than willing to self-righteously pass judgment.

But we must not blame ourselves. For whatever reason, our kids may have felt insecure one day at a party with friends or at a ball game or at an overnight bonfire or any other random place we trusted them to go. Or perhaps they were bored and wanted to try something new. Maybe peers pressured them or maybe they wanted to take a walk on the wild side just for fun. Maybe they wanted to be popular. Or maybe they were lulled by the promise of easy weight loss or a way to stay up to study for their final exams.

There are as many reasons to try drugs as not. And no drug addict ever said, "I think I'll go use drugs because I have such horrible parents." They were offered a joint, a pill, a pipe or a bottle and they made a tragic, ignorant, stupid, bad choice to try it. It felt good so they tried it again. The third time was no longer a choice. Addiction, which plays for keeps, had them.

CRITICAL BLOWS

Sandee's Story

My nightmare began five years ago. At the time, I had temporary joint custody of Cam, my three-month-old grandson due to domestic violence between my son and his wife. It had become so bad they separated; and within a very short time, my son found another woman and moved in with her.

One night while Cam was asleep in his crib, I received an alarming phone call informing me my daughter-in-law, Cam's mother, had been in a fatal car accident. This was the first of many critical blows we received. The suddenness of her death was a complete shock, while my heart broke for the sweet baby who no longer had his mother. Even though my son had been separated from his wife for three months, he was devastated over her death. I couldn't help but worry how this would affect custody of the baby. So the next day, my son and I called a lawyer who told us my son would automatically receive full custody. Cam would now join his father and girlfriend, who had two young girls of her own. They were only three miles away, so happily, he could still stay with me most days while my son worked.

About a month after my daughter-in-law's death, my son and his girlfriend had an argument and she left him. He was distraught and asked me to take Cam for a few days. But on the evening of the third day I received a call from him and he sounded very strange. He said his girlfriend and her daughters were back at the apartment and there was about to be trouble. Before I could even ask what he meant, the phone line went dead. I tried calling him back, but there was no answer. I was home alone with Cam and my two five-year-old daughters and was so worried I had no choice but to quickly load them into the car and drive to his apartment.

He was there waiting for me as I pulled up. He opened the car door, removed Cam from his car seat and carried him inside. I followed him with the girls through the front door when I noticed there was no front door. It had been broken down. When I called out to him to ask about the door, his response was his girlfriend had locked him out of the apartment. He was acting so strange. He was shaking and talking so fast his words were jumbled together and I could barely understand him. He handed Cam to me and said he needed to teach his girlfriend a lesson for locking him out. Still holding Cam, I followed him further into the apartment. He had disappeared into the laundry room, was beating the dryer with his fists and cursing his girlfriend who was nowhere to be seen. "Her girls are next!" he yelled. At that moment, instinct took over and I ran into their room to protect them. But no one was there. No one was anywhere in the apartment. We were alone.

It was then I realized he must have been hallucinating and I demanded to know what drug or combination of drugs he was taking. While shaking with anger, he started cursing me, something he had never done in his life. He was yelling at me to hand him his baby. When I refused, he threatened me. I immediately retreated towards the car and told my girls to get in quickly. Once we were all in the car, I locked the doors and hurriedly buckled their car seats. I tried to stay calm while I drove to a place where I could safely park the car and call his ex-girlfriend. I asked her if she had been at the apartment earlier that day. She responded she hadn't been back since she left him three days ago.

I was terrified leaving him there alone. But there was no way I could subject the children to his violent behavior, so I asked my eldest son to check on his brother. Upon arriving there, he found his younger brother still hallucinating and threatening to drive his car, so my eldest was forced to call the police. The police said they suspected my son was coming down off of methamphetamines and the best thing to do was to leave the premises, let him crash and sleep it off.

I had heard about the evils of meth, but really knew very little about it. In my mind, meth was something that "others" did, not my son. He was the sweetest, most loving person. Since childhood, we were always the closest of all my kids. I remembered during his preteen years how he hated cigarettes and drugs. He would pray every night that his grandmother would quit smoking.

So what happened? How could he have possibly gone in this direction? I felt it had to somehow be my fault. What had I done to cause my son to become a drug addict? Night after night, I racked my brain for an answer. Could it have been his dad's and my divorce? He was only four years old when we divorced. He had a good relationship with his dad and visited him every other weekend. In fact, it was actually my eldest son who had taken the divorce the hardest. Yet, he didn't do drugs of any kind, nor did my daughter who was only two years old when her father left.

Two years after the father of my first three children and I divorced; I married a wonderful man who became their generous and loving stepfather. Together we had another son and then twelve years later we adopted two baby girls from China. When we brought the girls home, my son was still living with us and became almost like a second dad to them. I always thought he would be an awesome father one day. But suddenly that changed. I no longer recognized my son.

His decision to choose drugs over his own precious child forced me to make the most difficult decision of my life. I went to juvenile court and filed for emergency temporary custody of my grandson. My heart ached when I thought about doing this to my son, but how could I not protect an innocent child? Putting my grandson first over my own son was the hardest thing I ever had to do.

The judge granted me temporary custody and on my way home from the courthouse, my son called to tell me he was coming over to the house to get Cam. I had to tell him I had just received custody. I felt like my heart was going to burst into a million pieces as he screamed into the phone I was stealing his child. I knew I was right to protect Cam from his father's violent drug-induced outbursts but I was still an emotional wreck. I put on a happy face during the day for my children and grandson. But once the kids were asleep, the tears began and wouldn't stop.

As if I didn't have enough family upheaval to deal with, my mother became an antagonist and made the situation with my son worse. Even though she previously encouraged me to get custody of Cam, she now began to take pity on my son. She was convinced no grandson of hers would do drugs. So when he was evicted from his apartment; she took him into her home. She paid for everything he needed, which included hiring an expensive lawyer in order to fight me for custody of Cam. My own mother had turned her back on me and was fighting for her drug-addicted grandson. I tried telling her many times he might be her grandson, but he was still an addict and would eventually steal from her. But she refused to believe me.

By this time I realized no matter what I did; nothing was in my control. I simply couldn't take another blow to my life. I grieved until I couldn't take it anymore and one night I finally gave it all to God. I knew God loved my son even more than I did and I needed to hand control over to Him. It was the hardest prayer I ever prayed but I asked him to do whatever was needed to stop my son, even if it meant jail time.

My prayer was quickly answered. Early the next morning my son called to say he had been arrested for manufacturing methamphetamines. After telling him I wouldn't bail him out of jail, I called my mother to tell her about my prayer the night before in hopes it would make a difference. I told her I believed God was watching over our family and begged her to please not post the money for bail. "Don't tell me what to do," she replied and went straight to his rescue. She posted bond and brought him home with her. She hired the best lawyer in town and all of his charges miraculously disappeared.

We continued going to court over custody, which kept my nerves on edge and my blood pressure high. On every court date, the judge saw through my son's pretense and ordered several hair follicle drug screens. But purposely, my son always kept his head and the rest of his body shaved causing the tests to be inconclusive.

I'll always remember the irony of the day my mother called me in tears, saying her heirloom jewelry was missing. Even though I had specifically warned her, my heart still broke my son could steal from his grandmother. I was ultimately hoping his upbringing could win out over the drugs. Still, he played the charade worthy of an Academy Award, as he cried and consoled my mother and promised her he would find the culprit. He even cooperated with and encouraged the police to find the thief. It was amazingly convincing. Eventually the detective on the case traced the jewelry back to his girlfriend. As soon as she was arrested, she sang like a canary and told them my son was also involved. He turned himself in and took all the blame. My son received two years probation but never went to jail, even though my mother surprisingly agreed to press charges.

With his court issues over, he was able to file for custody of his son. However, he had no job, no vehicle and no home so he moved in with his dad and nothing has changed. I am so sad about my son. He just turned thirty years old and has lost everything due to the consequences of his poor choices. There is nothing I can do for him. At least we continue to be there for his son.

BATTLE CRY

By definition, codependency is a dysfunctional relationship that is often one-sided and very controlling. This can be detrimental to both parties and can hinder recovery. It is a trap. The codependent is under the mistaken assumption he or she can fix anything. Don't be fooled. It doesn't work that way.

Codependency is an enemy, which must be acknowledged and stopped for healthy relationships to exist. Only by getting out of the way of the addict do they have a chance at finding recovery. As much as we desperately want sobriety for our loved ones, they have to want it more. It's freeing when we can finally see that. There has to come a point where we say, "enough" and that becomes our battle cry.

Janice 's Story

My son is a drug addict. Not surprisingly, his girlfriend is also a drug addict. But my story didn't really begin until we had to face the terrifying reality she was pregnant.

Our beautiful granddaughter came to live with us when she was just five months old. The road to gaining custody of her was paved with extreme stress and anxiety forming the cobblestones of uncountable sleepless nights.

As a skilled enabler, I firmly believed I could fix anything and allowed my son and his girlfriend to move into our home. I was sure I could keep her from using drugs during her pregnancy and therefore protect the baby. It quickly became clear I was wrong. When she finally went to the doctor, she was already six months along and the doctor decided to conduct a drug test. Testing positive for meth and he reported her to Child Protective Services (CPS).

When CPS opened her case, we were not prepared for what we were about to learn. She previously had three other children who had been removed from her custody. They had been put up for adoption by the state because of neglect, child endangerment and abandonment. We were sick after hearing this revelation but discovered this was not news to my son. Over the next few months, his girlfriend rarely went to the doctor. CPS notified the local hospitals to flag her so wherever she delivered, the baby would be tested for drugs. Fortunately, the knowledge they would be testing was enough to keep her off drugs as her due date approached.

As soon as Jaycee, our beautiful granddaughter was delivered, the nurse conducted a drug test on both mother and baby. During their three-day hospital stay, while awaiting the test results, my husband and I set up a trailer for them in which to live. They had nothing, so we filled the cabinets and refrigerator with food and made it infant-ready. The drug tests came back negative, thrilling us beyond words and they were both discharged from the hospital. But it didn't take long for old habits to resurface.

Every day I brought my infant granddaughter back to our home to help care for her. She would always be dirty and in the same clothes I had taken her home in the day before. I would bathe her and put powder and lotion on her tiny body. When it was time to take her back, I would cry. Many times, when I arrived at the trailer, her parents would both be sleeping. I'd see soiled diapers all over the floor, dirty dishes piled high in the sink and clothes scattered on the couch and floor. I was so distraught seeing this but knew there was nothing I could do. If her mom was awake when I got there, she'd take Jaycee from the car seat and put her right back to bed. I never saw her play with the baby. They seemed to stay up all night drinking and using drugs and then slept all day. I'd receive continuous calls because they needed formula or diapers, which I would always provide. I was more than happy to provide the formula because I felt it was better for the baby. I was afraid our granddaughter would ingest drugs through breast milk.

CPS attempted to make regular visits. But many times, no one would answer the door and then the caseworker would come to our house. On one occasion, the CPS worker became so concerned about the situation she asked us if we would be prepared to take custody of the baby. Without giving it a second thought we said "yes" and they immediately began to do our criminal background checks. We hoped the checks would be completed quickly as we couldn't stand seeing our granddaughter living under those conditions.

Due to neglect, Jaycee had sores under her arms, under her chin and behind her ears from spitting-up or sweating and then never being wiped dry. I would clean and put medication on them and then have to send her back home again and the process would repeat. It made me heartsick every time I had to drop her off. I never knew what to expect amidst the chaos.

Just one example of the nightmare we faced took place when Jaycee was two months old. My husband and I had taken care of her while my son and her mom went out. Around ten o'clock that night, we got a call from our son saying that Jaycee's mom was coming to get her. He pleaded with us not to let her leave with the baby because she was angry and drunk. I told him we didn't have the authority to keep her from taking Jaycee and that he needed to leave the bar where he was and come to our house immediately. He refused, saying he was in the middle of a dart tournament.

Jaycee's mother showed up shortly after the call, took our granddaughter from my arms, put her in the carrier without a coat or a blanket and proceeded to walk away. There were several feet of snow on the ground. I tried to stop her but she kept walking so I called the sheriff's office. Meanwhile, I jumped in the car to go after them and that's when I saw her literally crawling over a huge snowdrift. The baby was screaming. I finally convinced her to just get into the vehicle and let me drive. I promised to take her any- where she wanted to go. She said to take her to her grandmother's, which I did.

When I got home, the sheriff was waiting for me and I told him what happened. He explained there was nothing he could do since the baby was delivered somewhere safely. He did, however, tell me he would make a report and it would go to CPS along with all the others they had on file.

The night we finally got custody of our granddaughter was a continuation of the unbelievable drama we had been facing. Her mom had taken her to a known local drug house. My son called and asked me to go get the baby. I told him I would go as long as he called the sheriff's office. By the time I got to the drug house, there were two sheriff cars parked outside. One policeman was talking to my son while the other was talking to his girlfriend, sepa- rately. A third policeman was on the phone with a CPS worker, who told him to send the baby home with me.

I took Jaycee home. Almost immediately, CPS called and ad- vised me to take Jaycee to the courthouse the next day, file for emergency temporary guardianship and not to leave the court-house until the judge signed the order. The next morning, we did just that. I filled out the paperwork, filed it and waited for the judge. We sat and waited all day long. Just as the court was about to close for the day, the judge signed the order. We took our grand-daughter home, finally feeling secure we wouldn't have to release her back to her parents. Two months later, we received full legal guardianship.

That was almost seven years ago. After receiving guardianship, we allowed supervised visits for my son and his girlfriend. Many times they would come to see her and fall asleep during the visit, pretending to be sleeping with Jaycee while she napped. A year later, her mom got pregnant again with my son's child. This time we chose not to get attached. We knew at some point this baby would also be removed and decided we could not raise another child. This was an extremely difficult and truly heart-wrenching decision for us to make. But at the time, we felt it was in everyone's best interest.

By the time this new baby was born, my son and his girlfriend were no longer together. She took the baby and left the area. Before leaving town, we did get to see our youngest grandchild, another girl, a few times and Jaycee also got to see her baby sister. That was four years ago and no one has seen her mother since. We heard she not only ended up losing that child, but also cus-tody of two more children. Gratefully, another family adopted our youngest granddaughter. I tell myself every day, that sweet baby is where she is supposed to be and hope someday we can be reunited so Jaycee will have the opportunity to have a relation-ship with her sister.

Our journey has not been easy, to say the least, but is one I wouldn't trade for anything in the world. Yes, we have lost many of our retirement years to doing things younger parents normally do such as homework and after-school activities. But we truly believe it is the life that we were meant to have. We have done what is necessary to make sure our precious granddaughter receives everything she could possibly need. She knows without question she is loved.

Our son is in and out of her life depending on where he is in his addiction. If he is sober and clean, we allow him to be a part of it. Jaycee loves him and cherishes the time she gets to spend with him. She rarely speaks of her biological mom and hardly remembers her, which to some degree is a blessing.

I truly feel sorry for both my son and Jaycee's mom for what they have lost. They have missed every significant milestone in her life and have not been present for any of those special "firsts." It makes me happy I don't have to miss these times with this beautiful, healthy, happy child who brings so much joy to our lives. In spite of everything and maybe even because of it, we feel we are blessed.

CASUALTIES ACCEPTED

Denial and enabling, together, are as much an integral part of being the parent of an addict as drugs are to the addict. We want so much to believe we're not seeing what is right in front of us, especially when young children are involved. When we do, we try to help as much as possible. But because of the laws protecting bio parents and children, we are many times at an impasse.

Cathy's Story

I never thought I would be raising kids in my fifties nor did I ever think I'd be an addict's mom. My husband and I did everything we could to raise responsible kids, yet our first-born son became an addict.

My eldest son started a family at a very young age. He and his wife and their four beautiful children shared ownership of a house with her mother, but his life always seemed to be in turmoil, which caused us great concern. They were always fighting and would be up all night. When my son went to work, his wife slept all day. We thought they were simply having marital issues and many times, we stepped in to help with the kids hoping they would be able to work things out. Living with her mother and not getting along, created so much stress that sometimes it necessitated their living with us.

During this chaotic time, their marriage continued to suffer and my daughter-in-law eventually left my son and moved back in with her mother. Soon after, they began to work on their relationship again and my son returned to his wife, but it didn't last and the trouble continued.

After three years of this insanity, thinking their ongoing disharmony was simply marital issues; my husband and I finally had enough and suggested we take temporary guardianship of the children. We thought maybe my son and his wife might find it easier to focus on working out their problems without the responsibility of the children. But they refused our offer.

Around the same time, I received a strange call from one of my son's high school friends who wanted to talk with us regarding our son. I couldn't imagine what this could be about and was utterly shocked when he revealed our son had been using cocaine for many years and had recently gotten into something really bad called "cheese."

"Cheese?" I told him I had just heard something about that on our local news. I believed it to be some kind of heroin derivative. My son's friend continued on to explain that medications like Tylenol PM are crushed up, mixed with heroin and snorted. Oh my God. He was telling me that my son was a heroin addict. Heroin? Was he kidding me?

The next day, though still stunned, I confronted my son and he admitted to using. He insisted he and his wife were trying to get off of it but couldn't do it on their own. Giving me a bit of relief, he asked us for help and we eagerly agreed. All six of them immediately moved back into our house, while we helped them through detox and got them into a program. For a while, they seemed to be doing great. They were both clear-headed and talking about the future. Things were looking good so they decided to move back into their house with her mother. They promptly relapsed. Once again, we welcomed them back into our home in hopes of helping them get back on track again.

I knew very little about heroin at that time. My son said they had only been doing it for three months and it wasn't even "straight" heroin, so in my mind it should have been easy to stop. Well, it didn't take long before I learned they had actually started shooting "straight" heroin. I had asked my son on several occasions if they were using again but he always denied it. How could I have been so blind? I should have been able to see the signs sooner. Alcoholism ran rampant through my bloodline. I grew up with it. My sister was an alcoholic/addict and I watched her behavior for years. I thought I would have been smart enough to not be so gullible. I loved him so much and just wanted to believe him. But now, I could see it. Along with their behavior, the cysts on my son and daughter-in-law's hands and arms immediately made sense and confirmed my suspicions. That's when I made the decision to ask them again to give us guardianship. I was doing most of the work with the kids, anyway. But it was no use.

Meanwhile, my son would drive the boys to school each day, come home and sleep until he had to go to work. When he started arriving later and later to work, it was downhill from there. One day, the boys came home from school and the oldest who was eight at the time, said that someone from Child Protective Services (CPS) had been talking to him and his brother at school.

What?

I was worried-sick over this news but even more concerned because my daughter-in-law was freaking out. I instantly reassured her we would get through it as a family. The following week, she and my son were called into the CPS office and were also instructed to bring the girls with them. That's when my phone rang with news that shook my world. My son and his wife had tested positive for opiates and the girls were being immediately removed from their care.

I was fifty-four years old and was suddenly entrusted with the care of four children, ages two, four, six and eight—the casualties of the war we were fighting. I know I previously asked for custody and truly believed it would be temporary. That certainly seemed unlikely now, and I felt like I was in over my head. Raising four children after raising two of my own was the last thing I ever dreamed I'd have to do at my age. But I told myself, I am a mom, after all, and I decided I was going to be the best mother I could be to these children. My husband and I love them with all our hearts and are their only stability and foundation. Together, we will always be there for them.

WAR GAMES

Betty's Story

"**W**hy are you so hostile? You are so stuck in the past. I feel sorry for you because you are going to have a lonely miserable life if you can't learn to forgive. Why can't you be supportive instead of always judging me? Why can't you just say you hope I learned from my mistakes?"

My answers?

"I am stuck in the past because the past never goes away. I am angry because I rallied behind you all those years hoping you would learn a lesson from your mistakes and finally grow in a different direction. I was supportive long after everyone else in the family gave up. How long am I supposed to hope you will turn yourself around? It's been twenty years. I don't want to be disappointed anymore."

My youngest daughter, age thirty, has been stealing and taking drugs since she was ten. I have had her in many rehabs and went through the entire juvenile justice system with her. She has stolen our cars, wrapped them around trees and was expelled from high school all because of drugs. I kicked her out of the house at age eighteen and she lived in her car. After a time, she somehow got a job, saved her money and was able to get an apartment. I thought she was finally headed in the right direction. Then her life blew apart once again, but this time she was pregnant.

Against my husband's wishes, I allowed her to come back home. After all, she was going to have a baby—our grandson. Bringing her home almost ruined our marriage. My husband was dead set against her coming back to our house. But I just couldn't allow her to be pregnant and out on the street.

She gave birth to our beautiful grandson. Since the bio dad was in prison and his family was non-existent in our grandson's life, with our help, she was finally on more stable ground. A few years later, she had a good job, a car and was even making enough money to get her own place. We began to feel hopeful that maybe this would really be the beginning of the end. We prayed that her son would be her priority. Surely she would stay on track because of him.

But it didn't stick and her life blew apart again. Child Protective Services (CPS) got involved because she had a drug dealer living with her. Our grandson was placed with us and our daughter wound up in jail. While she was there, we paid her rent and bills and once she got out, CPS gave her son back to her. She lived on unemployment for almost two years and hooked up with another guy who promised to give her everything she'd always wanted in life. He was so convincing that even we fell for it hook, line and sinker. We spent thousands of dollars helping them move into a rental house close to his job six hours away. We really thought that he was a good guy and that being supportive was the right thing to do.

However, after only three weeks, we got the call to come rescue her and our grandson. The boyfriend was strung out on meth and had lost his job. Our daughter was frantic because she was finding needles under the rug and afraid our grandson would discover them. My husband agreed to intervene and moved them back home with us. A few weeks later, the boyfriend showed up and unbelievably, she went back with him. He insisted on taking our grandson with them. Then she confessed to us that she was the one who got the boyfriend on meth in the first place and that it wasn't his fault.

I was devastated and immediately called CPS. I gave them leads as to where they might be, and luckily CPS was able to track them down. They removed our grandson from her again and placed him with us until we could figure out our next step. CPS told us they would have to put him into foster care, unless we wanted to seek custody.

We wasted no time, hired an attorney and were awarded guardianship. In Texas, we were able to do something called Managing Conservatorship. In this case, the parents do not relinquish their parental rights, but maintain the option of someday petitioning the court to get custody back. However, they must prove singly or together they can provide a drug-free, violence free, stable and safe environment for the child. We opted to go that direction in order to provide an incentive for one or the other parent to clean up their act. Plus the attorney said it was easier to get the parents to sign voluntarily because they retained some rights. We also wouldn't have the additional cost of having them subpoenaed to go before a judge in a formal court case. We were able to get them both to sign the documents because they knew this was best for their son. Shortly after, our daughter, the boyfriend and bio dad all wound up in prison on various felony convictions.

The words at the beginning of this story were the last ones my daughter and I said to each other before she was handcuffed and taken into custody. She has had many jail terms but this was the first prison sentence, so it felt different. It felt real. Maybe that was why the truth came out so brutally for both of us.

Hopefully, she better understands the consequences of her actions and the impact they have had on everyone. With any luck, this time she'll come away with a new determination to change and to start a new life. At least we were both able to hug and say, "I love you." I hope she realizes the magnitude of those words.

DIFFERENT ROADS

One would think that having an addicted child would be as much as any parent could handle. Dealing with the challenges they bring can consume a family and destroy it fiber by fiber. So it's almost unfathomable when some families are faced with two or even more children battling addiction. It doesn't matter how different they are, how similar or how often we may have had the best plans for them. There's a saying often heard in recovery groups: "God only gives you as much as you can handle." Sometimes we wish he didn't have quite so much faith in us.

Lynne's Story

Our two youngest children, different as night and day, succumbed to experimenting with drugs and once they started, they couldn't stop. Having one addict in the family was shocking enough, but two? Our son, an excellent student, started his drug career the summer before his senior year of high school. He convinced us it was just a phase and he'd stop as soon as he left for college. We hoped, because it was mostly just marijuana, this really was just a passing fancy.

Many times we'd visit him at college and, though he looked a bit off, we wanted so much to believe he was simply tired from studying; we let it go. Besides, we had just discovered that our daughter, also away at college, had gotten into cocaine.

We first became suspicious of her troubles during our phone calls. She couldn't remember what I'd just told her minutes before, her voice seemed unusually raspy and she was uncharacteristically talking a mile a minute. But the moment of truth came when her student loan money for tuition never showed up in her account. That's when my husband and I called various rehabs around town to gather information and seek options in case our notion was correct. We were told to surprise her with a drug test and be ready with an ultimatum.

After driving to her school, drug test in hand, she tested positive for cocaine. We were sick. Even though she denied the test's validity, she agreed to attend the nine-month outpatient rehab the counselor suggested. She enrolled in the program and even with a couple of relapses along the way, was looking forward to graduating. But as she was approaching the end of her rehab program, our son's addiction was worsening.

Besides marijuana, he had added ecstasy and other hallucinogens to his drug repertoire, and was also selling to maintain his habit. Getting arrested for being under the influence and the loss of his after-school job didn't stop him. Although he told us he was doing well at school and work, the drugs had taken over his life and he was no longer attending classes. How he made it to his senior year in college, we'll never know. But this was now at a halt. So on his birthday, we gave him an unexpected gift: either come in for rehab or lose our support.

Initially, he resisted our offer. A month later, we heard from him. He said he'd come in for treatment. We were elated. Although, unbeknownst to us, he had a different "plan" in mind. His strategy was to go through the motions of rehab just to make us happy, and then go back to his drugs. But something happened. He was at a speaker meeting at the outpatient treatment center and the speaker's talk resonated with him. We were sitting beside him at the same meeting and saw the change come over him. His face lit up as if a miracle had taken place. When the speaker ended his talk, our son looked at us and said, "That's my story."

The next day, he asked the speaker to be his sponsor and never looked back. Since that meeting, he has never waivered, never relapsed and has diligently worked his program. Today, he's over fifteen years sober. He sponsors other addicts and remains very involved with the recovery community.

Our experience with our two children on different roads was as diverse as they were. While our son found life in his sobriety, we later discovered our daughter used continuously during her recovery program. As often as our son tried to warn her that her actions were going to kill her—she didn't heed his warnings—and they finally did.

It seems like an eternity. Still, it's always there front and center as we raise our deceased addict daughter's son as our own. Aside from preparing him about what he "might" have to face in the future, we are fortunate to have our son in the wings as a role model of hope. He never would have become the empathetic, introspective, understanding, warm and loving person that he is, today, without his experience. He is our partner in raising our grandson to hopefully always be drug free. We are forever grateful for that miracle.

PRISONERS OF WAR

Jerri's Story

My husband and I have always made faith a priority in our lives and have put God first in everything we do. Consequently, we made every effort to raise our two daughters in the same manner. The girls participated in church activities from a very early age and appeared to willingly embrace our Christian values. But we learned the hard truth about free will. Being raised in a certain way does not guarantee a child's safety or necessarily deter them from making questionable choices that could ultimately devastate their future.

Our eldest daughter faced behavioral challenges from a very early age. She had Attention Deficit Disorder and was under the care of a psychologist for her behavioral issues. During high school, I was informed she also suffered from Oppositional Defiant Disorder, which explained many of our constant struggles with her since early childhood. I wanted so much for her to be "normal," I pretended everything was okay for as long as possible. But her life was far from normal.

As she got older we firmly stressed that dating was something that should not be rushed and naturally, she strongly disagreed. Even so, we were devastated and shocked when we discovered our daughter was pregnant at only fifteen years old. How could this be? We tried to convince her to give the baby up for adoption because we knew she was too young and immature to raise a child. However, we also lost that battle and had to accept our fate. She would be bringing a baby into our home.

She gave birth to a beautiful baby girl. We sincerely hoped that with our help, everything would go smoothly as we parented this child together. But when our granddaughter was just three years old, her mother met someone new and was introduced to Xanax, ecstasy and marijuana. She very quickly moved on to the more addictive cocaine and crystal meth.

As she spiraled downward in her drug haze, she was no longer able to care for her child, continue her studies or remain at her job. Still, we had confidence things would change. We had such high hopes for her. After all, before her dance with drugs, she had received her GED Certificate, started court-reporting school and was also working at a very good job. We ignorantly assumed as she matured, she'd stop using, return to parenting her child and go back to school. But that didn't happen.

Ten years later, she had four more children, all with different fathers. Along with her first daughter, we took over parenting her second child. She gave another up for adoption and one birth was twins, which her ex-husband chose to raise. Thankfully, she remained drug free during all her pregnancies and for almost two years after with every child. But when each of the babies got older and more complicated to raise, she relapsed and the vicious cycle returned.

My husband and I never imagined we'd be in the position of parenting our grandchildren because of drug addiction. When it happened, we held on to a foolish hope that it was "just a stage." We truly believed our daughter was not really a drug addict. We thought she would somehow outgrow her obvious problems with immaturity, wise up and return to parenting.

Still firmly entrenched in our state of denial, we got hit with another major setback. We learned our younger daughter had followed her sister into her dark lifestyle. This was so out of character for our second child, who had always been so compliant and a joy to have around with none of the behavioral challenges of her sister. But as she got older and began spending more time hanging around her older sister, everything began to change. At just nineteen years old, she gave birth to her first child. And once again, we assumed the parenting role for raising that child and ultimately gained custody of him.

Eight and one-half years later, she had another baby while using crystal meth for most of the pregnancy. During her ninth month, she admitted herself into a rehab facility. Her plan was to immediately give the baby up for adoption. But the birth father refused to support that decision so she brought the newborn back to the rehab and continued working on her program.

She was back in rehab only two days when suddenly she began to have trouble breathing. The rehab staff sent her back to the hospital where she was diagnosed with congestive heart failure. Her physician was convinced it was caused by crystal meth use during pregnancy. She had damaged her heart. Her cardiovascular physician warned her she should never become pregnant again and that any drug use in the future would most likely kill her.

These warnings seemed to work for a time. Our daughter returned to rehab and did not use drugs for her entire stay. In fact, she stayed clean for the next two and a half years. But the honeymoon didn't last. She relapsed again on meth and the vicious downward cycle returned.

One particular day, she left her little boy in the care of one of her girlfriends and didn't return. Her friend called the Department of Human Resources (DHR) and they called us. In accordance with their safety plan, the DHR representative asked if we would take custody of her child. We were shocked and disheartened to be back in this position, but faithfully and lovingly hugged our two and a half year-old grandson and took him home to live with us.

Needless to say, our family has been completely turned upside down. We honestly thought everything was finally running smoothly and that our daughter was doing well taking care of her baby. As far as we knew, she was drug-free, had a job she liked, was living in her own apartment and even had a relationship with her first-born son. But unbeknownst to us, that all changed when she unexpectedly lost her job and met a drug-abusing man who had just been released from prison. She denied all reasoning and returned to that sordid world of darkness with him. Our daughter had become a person we no longer knew.

Today, we are parents for a second time to four children who never asked to become prisoners of a war that wasn't theirs. From our older daughter is our eldest girl, who is eighteen and a thirteen year-old boy, whom we share custody with his paternal grandmother. From our younger daughter, we have an eleven year-old boy and two and a half year-old boy. These children have been such a blessing to us; I cannot even begin to describe what we feel. While never the path we ever dreamed we would take, they help to keep us young. We are thankful to God that He has given us the opportunity to raise them and honored to be entrusted with their upbringing.

We hold on to the hope one day our daughters will stop using drugs, reclaim their lives and begin a relationship with their children. Until that day comes, we are here to fill in the gap. We are confident the Lord is with us and goes before us, making a way for us to continue to raise these children. And yes, sometimes we get overwhelmed, but we would not trade our lives for anything.

AMBUSHED

The world of addiction and mental illness frequently go hand in hand. The Substance Abuse and Mental Health Services Administration reports that over 8.9 million persons have co-occurring disorders. Sometimes the illness is known. But it often goes undetected until triggered, somehow, or an addict in treatment is diagnosed. Many experience depression, anxiety, bipolar mood swings or other mental, emotional and behavioral issues and may choose to self-medicate in an attempt to feel normal. Adding addiction to mental illness is more problematic and becomes a dual diagnosis.

Julie's Story

I am the first to agree that in some cases, parents are a huge contributing factor to addiction. You know them—the cool parents—the parents who "party" with their kids. Then there are the kids born into full blown addicted households and it would seem there would be no way a child could possibly escape substance abuse problems growing up in that environment. Sadly, many do not.

But, then there are the so-called "normal" families in which one kid is addicted and the other isn't. So many theories exist as to why this happens. Yet, we still don't have a definitive answer. I'm not sure we ever will.

Unless we fell into the first two categories of parenting we couldn't really be blamed or blame ourselves for screwing up our addicted children's lives. The reality is sometimes they just manage to do that all on their own. When this happens, we find ourselves ambushed and in into a battle we didn't cause. All we can do is act as defensively as possible to protect ourselves. I wish I had come to that realization much earlier than I did.

My daughter, Emily, began experimenting with drugs at twelve years old. She had a baby, Kyler, when she was sixteen, whom we are raising. Then she tragically committed suicide at age twenty. My son Colton was ten years younger than his sister, so my son and grandson were closer in age than my own natural children. One would think it would be an advantage having two boys in a family so close in age. But we were still a blended family and like most blended families, there were difficulties to be overcome.

Colton was diagnosed early on as being emotionally disturbed. Not surprisingly, he resented that our grandson was living in our home. He was mad at the circumstances as well as all of us. He was especially hurt that his sister committed suicide on his tenth birthday. Her death had an extremely negative and lasting impact on him.

From age fifteen to seventeen, he spent time in juvenile detention for drugs and at eighteen, went to prison. When he was released, I really hoped that his prison experience would have somehow changed him for the better and he'd come back home and peacefully live with us again. But it didn't happen that way.

It hurt my heart to make him leave our home when things didn't work out but I felt I had to do my very best to bring Kyler up in a safe and loving environment. I felt he deserved that much.

Having two children in one family with substance abuse issues has been devastating and I couldn't help but feel like I've been under attack from all sides. But having Kyler in my life has helped me through these rough times. He is a normal, caring child who never asked to be in shoes many people would find difficult to wear, much less a small child.

Now nineteen, Colton is still struggling. I fear that the battle he has faced isn't over yet and that I can never truly let down my guard. I can only pray. I can only give him to God. I know there is nothing I can do to prevent future attacks and have learned to rest in the knowledge that whatever may happen; I know I've done my best.

SURPRISE ATTACK

Regardless of the circumstances, our addicted children are always with us—even when they aren't. We make a supreme effort to find a way to live as normally as possible, always knowing they are out there somewhere. We try not to think about them or the fact our worst-case scenario fears could come true. Then suddenly, without warning, there is a reminder of them—a scent in the air or a song on the radio or we see someone who looks like them—and the flood of emotions—and the fear returns. It's an unending cycle.

Laura's Story

We used to live in a sailing town. How I loved the nice summer days when we could look across the harbor and enjoy the magnificent, colorful sailboats that suddenly appeared as soon as the weather turned warm. I never wanted to learn to sail because I knew that it looked much prettier than it really was. I knew that sailing was horrendously hard work and boat maintenance expensive and time consuming; but I loved the concept and the vision of the sport.

In my spare time I enjoyed perusing the small nautical shops in town and often purchased the wood and brass home décor items that they sold so that I could create some of that nautical feeling in my home. I even liked the analogy of life being a lot like sailing. When things are going well and the wind is in your sails it's easy to just sail along and enjoy the breeze. But lose that wind, and suddenly the sails deflate and just hang there, and the boat completely stops. At that point the only choice is to either wait for the wind to return or drop the sails and start up a motor to return to shore.

Having an addicted child living on the streets is a lot like living on a sailboat. It's extremely difficult but you get into a routine and manage to sail along normally as if everything is ok and even enjoy the ride. But then something comes along that reminds you that everything is not ok—suddenly the wind is gone, the sails are down and life simply just stops. It happens when you least expect it.

I was in a clothing store recently and right in front of me was a darling outfit exactly the style my daughter would absolutely love. Wind stops. Sails are down. It was all I could do to manage to keep enough control so that the sales people weren't wondering why this lady was losing it in their store. It literally took everything I had in me to start my motor and continue on. The rest of the day was a total loss. It happens all the time.

She called my husband yesterday. She loves him. She misses him. She wants to come home. She doesn't need help. She won't get help. Stalemate. Winds stop. Sails are down. It's all he can do to make it through the evening. It's all I can do to make it through the evening.

Today the winds are up and we are sailing again.

Until the next time.

II

INNOCENT SURVIVORS

⌒

"When I was very young, most of my childhood
heroes wore capes, flew through the air, or
picked up buildings with one arm. They were
spectacular and got a lot of attention. But
as I grew, my heroes changed, so that now
I can honestly say that anyone who does
anything to help a child is a hero to me."

—*Fred Rogers*

SAVING A CHILD

Lynne's Story

She gave birth to a child who would save her from
 The insane existence her life had become.
We hoped, as did she, this would be the key
 To keep her on track so that she could just be
A mother to her child, free of drugs at last;
She'd finally get help, put it all in the past.

"I can do it myself," she said righteously.
"We'll be just fine, my sweet baby and me."
 But reality brought on her sudden collapse
 And it took no time at all for her to relapse.
Forgetting her baby who needed her sober
She again chased the high; her addiction took over.

"We'll care for your baby until you get well."
Saw her hold back the tears then go back into hell.
But her time never came and with each passing year
Our dear grandson grew older with no mother near.
His father was also not present you see
And became clear to all; it would just be us three.

A ten-year battle bought our daughter her wings
As heart breaking as it is, to talk of these things.
But such is the case when there is addiction
Making real a tale we wish was just fiction.
Yet saving his life, we will never regret
For we thrive in the love we give and we get.

Sure, our lives are changed; we'll never be the same
Discipline, homework and all those baseball games.
Doing it, again, unlike in younger days
Past experience helps through the child-rearing maze.
Yes, an ache or a pain can put us in our place
But the blessing in return—the smile on his face.

Losing our daughter was not part of the plan
Forever we're changed, especially our clan.
To adopt this precious lad was best for our boy
He's now safe in the world and this fills us with joy.
Our lives are now different but we're more than okay
Because our child is happy and thriving each day.

SAFE HAVEN

The tragic reality of the drug world too often means children must experience incomprehensible hardship. This comes as a result of their parent's decisions before steps can be taken to rescue them. As grandparents, saving them is our most important mission even if it means we have to go into active battle and fight for them.

The fragility, egos and stubbornness of our addict children causes stress and havoc in our lives as we struggle to keep peace with them. Even in recovery, it takes time—sometimes years—for them to be capable of parenting.

But, the agonizing decision to put what's best for a grandchild before a child is a mother's greatest tragedy. It's something we never imagined we'd have to do. We fought for our addict children until we realized it could no longer be our battle. Left along the way in all the turmoil and rubble, were our innocent grandchildren and it became our destiny to champion these precious children who could not do it alone.

Patti's Story

My daughter has battled addiction for as far back as I can remember and has tried unsuccessfully numerous times to get clean. So during intake for her fifth attempt at rehab, it was quite a shock when her urine sample showed she was not only clean, but she was also very pregnant. A check-up revealed she was actually five months along. Being so far into her pregnancy meant her only choice, aside from keeping the baby, was to put it up for adoption. After a great deal of discussion, we both agreed she should keep the baby. But I had so many mixed emotions, especially because this was so clearly not what she needed at this time of her life. Deep down inside I couldn't deny the nagging thought I was going to be raising her baby.

Our daughter stayed with us for a while. But then she told the alleged father of the baby she was pregnant and decided to move in with him. She promised after the baby's birth, she would come stay with us until the baby was six weeks old. When she went into labor, I accompanied her to the hospital and was in the delivery room when she gave birth to a healthy, beautiful baby girl. As planned, mom and baby both came home with me when they were released from the hospital. But something wasn't right.

Two weeks after the birth, my daughter's attitude and behavior seemed off. I couldn't explain what I felt but red flags were going up. Could she be thinking of going back to drugs? At four weeks, she told me I was too controlling and accused me of trying to steal her baby. She said she needed to leave. Just short of six weeks, she moved back in with the baby's daddy.

But their life together was far from stable. The baby's daddy called me daily and informed me my daughter wanted to use drugs and complained she wasn't feeding the baby enough. He said the baby was always crying and seemed hungry. He tried to watch while she fed the baby but my daughter would lock him out of the bedroom so he could never tell how much she was actually feeding her. He was perplexed. He had no understanding about addiction and was always criticizing my daughter's mothering. So it surprised me, when one day, they told us they wanted some time alone and asked me if I would watch the baby for the night.

Of course I said yes. But fifteen minutes after dropping the baby off, my daughter asked her boyfriend to drop her somewhere downtown. He refused and he drove her back to their apartment, arguing the entire ride. Once they arrived, she jumped out of the car and took off to look for drugs. She was gone for three days. After returning to their apartment to sleep it off, she asked him to bring her to our home to pick up the baby. I told my daughter if she wasn't done doing drugs, to leave the infant with me. She insisted she was done and they both grabbed the baby and left.

By the end of that week, her boyfriend called me in a panic. He said my daughter wanted money for drugs and when he refused, she started beating him. The police were called and my daughter was arrested for domestic violence. That's when the daddy felt he had no choice but to bring the baby to me. He said he didn't know what else to do. I held the baby and assured him I'd take care of the child.

Based on the police report stating an infant was involved, Social Services had to open a case. After my husband and I passed background checks and had our home inspected, we were granted temporary custody. We thought we could finally relax. However, by the baby's first birthday, the dad decided he wanted custody. Distraught but determined, we fought with him for over a year; but we lost. Our happy, healthy almost two-year-old little granddaughter was suddenly leaving us. I was a mess and my husband was also depressed. The baby held on tight and didn't want to leave my arms. How could he be awarded full custody while my daughter's parental rights were completely taken away? And what about us?

The day he came for the baby he said we could visit with her for only a few hours once a week. Hearing this, I broke down and was totally devastated he would withhold this baby from us when I was the only mommy she knew. Fortunately, the dad had a good friend who convinced him not to do this to us or to her. Astoundingly, he agreed and a month after he was awarded custody, our little doll baby was returned to us and has been ours ever since.

Our granddaughter's life is now one of safety and stability. Her daddy picks her up on Saturday mornings for scheduled visits and returns her on Sunday evenings. She is a very happy four and one-half-year-old, attends preschool part-time, will start kindergarten in September and loves going to dance class two nights a week. She is smart, funny, creative and well behaved. Luckily, we have seen no signs of ill effects from the drugs my daughter used during her early months of pregnancy.

It has been a different journey, however, for my daughter. For the first three years, she was in and out of my granddaughter's life so she knows her birth mommy. But the last time she saw her mommy was on her third birthday. My daughter stayed clean for three weeks before the big birthday bash. Then three days later she was gone.

This was a big turning point for me. I knew I was done and realized it was time for me to let my daughter go. As moms, we are forever caretakers. We naturally want to fix boo-boos and make everything all better. But with addiction we have absolutely no control. The irony is the sooner we are able to let go and understand there is really nothing we can do, the sooner we can begin to heal. It took a lot of time for me to get to that place. I had cushioned my daughter's falls for so many years thinking it was my job and believing each time would be the last time.

But unexpectedly, I had an innocent child in my care that needed me to be whole—not a shell of a woman walking in the shadow of my daughter's addiction. I'm sure my daughter still thinks I received what she always thought I wanted—her child. In reality, this couldn't be further from the truth. I'd much rather, with all of my heart, be just a regular grandma. But I didn't get that choice.

After a great deal of thought, I finally got up the courage and told my daughter when she was working a program and had one year clean, I'd be willing to bring her back into our lives, but not before. I was also able to get the baby's daddy to agree with me to not allow her near the baby until then. I knew I could trust him not to subject the child to her mommy's insanity.

I have not spoken to my daughter in over a year and do not know anything about her life. The exception is when she's in jail because I still check online almost daily to see if she's been arrested. Even though, for the most part I let her go, I still love my daughter and can't stop myself from continuing to search for any positive sign I can find. A small ray of hope for her remains within me and I won't give up until she finally gets well.

Of course, there are days I feel sadness about the choices she made that brought us to this point. But then I look at my life and the sadness disappears when I realize how much good I'm doing for my granddaughter and how much joy she has brought to us. Even my husband loves her like she's his own. She is the light of our lives and she is her dad's little princess. I truly believe God gave this child to us so I could learn to detach with love from my daughter, allow Him to be in control and give my granddaughter the special life she deserves.

RESCUE MISSION

Pattee's Story

I'll never forget the morning my four-year-old granddaughter called me in a tremulous voice to tell me she couldn't wake her mama who was in bed with two men. I jumped into my car and was there within minutes to find it to be true. My daughter was passed out on the bed with two men, all fully clothed. My granddaughter's baby brothers, a two-year-old and an infant, were in their bedroom. I quickly gathered up all of my grandchildren and took them to my house.

This was just one of many bizarre episodes that had become all too commonplace over the years. My daughter was only fourteen years old when she started using drugs. She began with Sudafed, marijuana, alcohol and inhalants and moved on to crack and methamphetamines. By age eighteen, she had become so disrespectful and violent; I had no choice but to make her leave my home. It broke my heart.

Then I heard from her. She was pregnant and wanted to come home. She assumed her current boyfriend was the father but she had become pregnant from a one-night stand before this new relationship. Her boyfriend was furious and she didn't feel she could stay with him.

We allowed her to return home on the condition she would get help through counseling or drug treatment and she also agreed to either go to college or get a job. She accepted our terms and apologized tearfully. She lived with us and went to school and counseling. And amazingly, as far as we could tell, our daughter seemed to have pulled it all together and soon gave birth to her baby girl.

The next day she was discharged and she and the baby returned home with me. Initially, my daughter slept a lot, so I spent many nights in the living room with my granddaughter on my chest listening to classical music. As I held her gently and felt her tiny heart beating against mine, I vowed I would protect my precious grandchild from that day forward.

But sadly, with baby in tow, my daughter soon moved back in with her boyfriend. I watched helplessly over the next couple of years as constant violence coupled with police intervention took over her life due to her boyfriend's cocaine use. Amid the chaos, my daughter gave birth to another child, a little boy, two years after the first.

There had been so much violence and so many arrests CPS threatened to take the children away from her if she didn't remove the children from that environment. So in an effort to save her children, she broke up with him and moved in with a new man. Not surprisingly, this decision didn't turn out to be any better. The new boyfriend was addicted to Vicodin and was severely suicidal. Realizing she couldn't live with him either, she decided to move out. He was so distraught; he attempted to hang himself, as a result. She found him clinging to life and called 911.

Immediately after he survived his unsuccessful suicide attempt, she found out she was pregnant with baby number three and they moved back in together. But she did not want another child and tried unsuccessfully several times to abort the baby, until it was too late.

Before her pregnancy, my daughter had put herself on a waiting list for an eighteen-month-long nursing program and finally was accepted. But the first day of the program was also the day she gave birth to her third child, another son. Fortunately, she was excused for the first two days and began the program on day three.

The father of her third baby acted as step-dad to her other two children and stayed home to care for them. He cooked, cleaned and said prayers at night with them. But his Vicodin addiction was getting worse. Whenever we'd see him, he was glassy-eyed and often sweating even while wearing light summer clothing in the winter. Along with periodic episodes of anger, paranoia and moodiness, his behavior led to frequent break-ups, and their live-in relationship again ended.

My daughter moved into her own place and worked most weeknights as a nurse. But in order to help make ends meet, and regardless of our significant misgivings, she began freelancing as a pole dancer and escort on weekends. We'd help babysit so she could work and the kids spent many nights at our house.

A questionable relationship with one of her wealthy clients led her into getting cosmetic surgery for which she was prescribed Vicodin. At this point, the father of baby number three had moved in again to help care for her. He not only over-medicated her, but also stole her pills regularly, along with her money. With the stolen cash, he bought more pills on the street for his own addiction.

We weren't sure but believed the medication, along with the deceit, drove her back into the world of drugs. Soon after, she got fired from her job and then disappeared for two weeks. Luckily, the children were staying with us. Still, we were surprised when we didn't hear from her for the entire two weeks. This was uncharacteristic. She had always missed her children dearly when away from them and would even call from work each night to check on them. She worried about our driving skills whenever we took them on an adventure. She even questioned the details of our schedule including where we were going and when we would return. Of course, that was when she was healthy.

When my daughter finally surfaced, she came to get her children. I was sick with worry when I saw her. She was clearly high with her head wobbling and eyes blurry. I knew I had no power to prevent it and could only watch as she put them in her car and drove off with them at high speed. I was terrified. The next day, I wasted no time and consulted an attorney. But that afternoon she showed up unannounced and left the children with us once again. I was relieved they were safe with us and consequently, and very unwisely, put off taking court action. The following week, she returned to gather her children. I had no recourse. They were her children and my hands were tied. I could do nothing to protect them.

Over the next few years, almost daily, I'd get phone calls from my frightened granddaughter she could not wake her mother or stepfather in the mornings. She took on the responsibility to wake and dress her brothers—who wouldn't cooperate—get them breakfast and make their lunches. But she had no way to get them all to school because she attended a different school for gifted and talented children across town.

As soon as I heard her voice, I would drop what I was doing and rush over to help. I began to pack lunches for them ahead of time at my house so that I was ready to fly out the door as soon as my granddaughter called. It was absurd. I had to drive clear across town to get my daughter's children ready for school on time, yet I couldn't get myself ready for work or even eat breakfast. But I felt I had no choice. If I stopped, it would be my grandchildren who would be hurt.

The situation continued to deteriorate as my daughter began to truly neglect the children. They would either be left with others to care for them or abandoned for many hours while the adults retreated to other areas of the house behind locked doors. The kids said they saw fighting and peeked through a door crack and saw adults smoking something in the back room. For so many years I felt like they were on a horrible merry-go-round with no escape but I had no power legally to do anything. All I could do was to stay close by, monitor the situation and get involved when necessary.

I began to ask questions of people who knew my daughter and was shocked at what I discovered. I was told she had a friend frequently bring a drug dealer to her home in the middle of the night while the kids were sleeping. By this time, they were staying with us most nights of the week. But on this particular night they were with their mother. Her drug dealer stole money from her, and when she discovered this, she confronted him in her hallway right outside their bedroom door. He pulled a knife on her and she wrestled him to the ground. He was arrested.

Finally, that was it. I decided it was time for me to permanently intervene. In addition, the children reported multiple incidents of physical abuse and were clearly severely traumatized emotionally. They told me they didn't think their mother loved them anymore. I volunteered to care for them rather than risk their safety. But as my daughter began to disappear from their lives for longer and longer periods of time, I realized I had to get legal help. This time, I retained an attorney so I could move towards guardianship of my three grandchildren.

At that time, the State of California in its infinite wisdom, had recently revised laws allowing an available and willing parent to take a child out of an intact sibling unit, if the parent so desired.

With that, our middle little boy, who was already reeling from the loss of his stepfather and now mother, was plucked from our home and taken to a new home with his bio father, wife and two other children. Even though the father agreed to a fifty-fifty arrangement with us, he changed his mind and permitted him to be with us only on weekends.

Each weekend, our grandson would tell me how unhappy he was, especially when he was slapped or his ears were pulled or when his new parents spanked their infant. His father also kept him from attending the same gifted and talented program his sister attended. Although a bit more stable in his married life, the father still had domestic violence issues. Once our grandson told us things were a little bit better because "Dad hasn't thrown any TV's around lately." He also said he often prayed for God to make it possible for him to live with us. But sadly, I knew if I reported what he told us, we would undoubtedly lose all contact. So we chose to provide the best buffer we could for him with ongoing monitoring, love and support.

Our official permanent guardianship was granted for two of our grandchildren, but we continue to parent and love our middle grandson. My daughter did not come to the hearing, but instead went out-of-state into a drug detox facility. However, as soon as she heard the word "permanent," she immediately left the rehab. Inadvertently, my being awarded permanent guardianship may have hastened her drug use because I took the kids off her hands. This allowed her to be freely on the prowl all the time.

Unfortunately, my daughter has had very little to do with her children, insisting I took them from her. Even though I have told her numerous times over the years I did not want to raise her kids, she maintained I wanted to be their mother. She told me they are mine now. I could never comprehend her thinking or her unreasonable accusations. After all, she's the one who chose to go back to drugs and abandon her children.

We initially thought we would care for the children and keep them safe for maybe a year or two while our daughter straightened out her life. But we were faced with the undeniable reality of raising another family. The children are now ten, nine and six years old and have a long road ahead. I love them dearly. But my heart breaks for them and I know I cannot buffer my grandchildren from the trauma of having a mother who has forgotten them. She said it always hurts her too much to see them and so she never does. Like many addicts, this is a completely self-centered thought. The drugs have replaced her children.

Sometimes, I feel like my normal middle class educated family has been transported to and trapped on a bizarre island of strange aliens from which we can never escape. This is the insanity of the world of drugs and not a world I would ever have chosen to know. Like prisoners of a tragic war, we vow to do everything in our power to keep our grandchildren safe and to love and protect them for the rest of our lives.

DIVIDE AND CONQUER

Most vulnerable of all the casualties of the drug war are the children. They may end up in foster care or children's homes separated from their siblings. By all rights, where they should be, is tucked in bed each night by their own nurturing, healthy parents.

Susan's Story

It breaks my heart that Erin, my beautiful daughter who had a comfortable life and promising career, was swallowed up by addiction. It certainly took me by surprise.

Erin started out as a responsible single mom for the first five years of her daughter, Mikayla's, life. The birth father was never involved so Erin had to be the breadwinner. When little Mikayla started kindergarten, Erin wanted to build a more stable career for their future and became a student at the Police Academy. Life was good for several years. But then she was injured at work and her life took an unanticipated turn. Her doctor prescribed OxyContin for the pain, which immediately propelled her into a full-blown addiction. After her refills ran out, she went from doctor to doctor for the pain meds until they also cut her off. That's when she met Elijah, another addict. With his help, she bought drugs off the street. She used Roxicodone, morphine, meth—anything else she could find to feed her burgeoning habit. In addition, he became her boyfriend and over the next few years, she and Elijah had three children—the last two were born severely drug-exposed.

Meanwhile, Erin was arrested for prescription medication fraud and sentenced to jail. The Department of Child Services (DCS) sent her eldest child, Mikayla to a children's home and put her other three children, Sophie, Micah and Samuel in foster care. I wanted custody of all four children. But when I tried to get custody of the three younger children, their father didn't want me to have them and DCS decided it would be best for them to remain in state custody. Because Mikayla had a different father who was never in the picture, my chances were better to receive custody of her and so I fought hard for nine months and eventually won. She had just turned fourteen years old. During my court battle for Mikayla, Elijah cleaned up and was granted custody of his three children.

After her time in jail, Erin went into a court-ordered drug rehab program and returned to Elijah and the children, but never gave any regard to completing the required permanency plan that was in place for her to follow. Once again, due to her violation of the plan, the three little ones went back into state custody.

Currently, Erin and Elijah are clean and working to get their children back. Erin also wants Mikayla to come back to live with her to complete the family. But Mikayla, who's been with me for over two years isn't in favor of this idea. She dislikes Elijah's violent behavior and cannot forgive her mother. Thankfully, she is working on these issues in therapy and her scheduled visits with her mother are slowly improving. Still, she says she doesn't want to leave me. "Nanny," she always says, "you're the only one who fought for me. I will never leave you."

Therapy is also helping me to stop questioning and blaming myself for what happened to my daughter as well as helping me be the best parent I can be for Mikayla. The bond she and I have is very special. I'm eternally grateful I could be there for her to make a difference in a life she never deserved to have. I just pray, God willing, my other grandchildren will someday be able to return to healthy parents, as well as be reunited with their sister and hope drugs will never again touch their lives.

STAND THE WATCH

Without a doubt, it is the responsibility of the parent to monitor their children's activities; and that doesn't change when they reach adolescence. In fact, adolescence is when they need it the most. The teenage years are probably the most terrifying time during parenting that we will ever face—again.

A teen survey, The National Survey on American Attitudes on Substance Abuse was conducted by CASAColumbia and QEV Analytics in 2012. This and past surveys have consistently found "family" is fundamental to keeping children away from tobacco, alcohol and illegal drugs. Teens, whose parents expressed disapproval of these substances, were significantly more likely not to use them than teens of parents who were more lax.

Almost half of American high school students in grades nine through twelve not only reported they knew a student who sold drugs at their school, but there was also a place on school grounds or near school where students were able to use drugs, drink or smoke during the school day without getting caught.

Along with places to use, accessibility to drugs has become easier. Aside from knowing someone who sells drugs, teens can walk into a convenience store or use the Internet to purchase drugs. Easy to purchase is synthetic marijuana, K2, Spice or synthetic cathinones, which are man-made chemicals related to amphetamines and sold as "bath salts" or "jewelry cleaner." The Internet has also provided an added means for teens to be influenced into using drugs. A surprising seventy-five percent of the teen respondents said seeing pictures on social media of their peers partying with alcohol and marijuana encouraged others to imitate them. Compared to teenagers who have never seen these images, those who have, were four times more likely to have used marijuana and more than three times likelier to use alcohol. So "digital" peer pressure has now joined "personal" peer pressure in playing a significant role in getting teens started on drugs and alcohol.

Julie's Story

Remember years ago, when TV stations aired a public service announcement that said, "Parents, it is ten o'clock—do you know where your children are?"

I felt that was kind of funny and it certainly didn't pertain to me, because I always thought I knew where my children were. Even today, as I tell my grandson/son, Kyler (while he sighs and rolls his eyes) to be home by a certain time, to take his cell phone and answer my calls, while asking him who he's going to be with; I know he does not understand the importance of these requests.

Being parents, we have to face the facts. Some of the parents of the children our kids come into contact with have substance problems. Their children are at greater risk for developing substance issues themselves. Peer pressure for our kids is tremendous. What if your child's friend manages to get some dope and offers it to your child? Will he be strong enough, educated enough to say no?

We now know that methamphetamine, probably the worst of the worst, has a ninety-eight percent addiction rate after only one use. Statistically, it is much easier for adolescents to get drugs than alcohol. They basically just want to fit in. So if their best friend says, "Hey, you gotta try this. It's really cool!" And if there are a bunch of other kids waiting to see the response, there is a pretty good chance your child will try it—just to fit in, just to be "cool."

As "un-cool" as we are to our children, we have to find a way to convince them to walk away, to never try drugs in the first place. Some kids will get this concept. Unfortunately, some won't.

My parents didn't have to convince me of much in that area. My father often told me if I ever did drugs, he would "beat me to death," and I believed him. I am not condoning child abuse, but sometimes fear is a healthy deterrent. You would think most parents want to keep their kids from using drugs. But what about parents who suspect or know that their children are using drugs and don't know what to do about it? And then, as incomprehensible as it sounds, there are parents who not only allow their children to use drugs but encourage it and will even share the drugs with them. Seriously? We're supposed to love and protect our children, but that scenario doesn't seem to fit in with "loving and protecting."

There were kids whom I knew were bad for my daughter and who would try to hang around my house. I was afraid they could influence her. I always felt a twinge of guilt as I ran these kids off, mainly because I often felt they probably had no one to be accountable to. I wanted to help them, but certainly not at the cost of my own family. Later I found out some of these kids' parents condoned and participated in this behavior with their kids, and mine. As hard as I try to be forgiving about this, there is still a part of me that wants my father to "beat them to death."

My daughter first tried marijuana at the tender age of twelve. A man, who still lives across the street from the local junior high school, gave it to her. As much as I suspected illegal drugs were available on high school campuses, it never occurred to me that it could happen at the junior high level. That first act started her on a downward spiral from which she was never able to recover and ultimately she lost her life. There are people out there who do not have the best interests of our children at heart.

We need to know where are children are and who they are with. We need to educate our children about drugs. Opening a dialogue with them truly can save their lives.

GUARDIANSHIP FIGHTER

Saving our grandchildren can be done without legal means. But doing it legally will protect the rights of both child and grandparent. Several options (under different names depending on the state) such as legal guardianship, kinship care, foster care or adoption are available in order to gain authority to register the child for school, sports, etc. and get proper medical care.

With the exception of adoption, guardianship of a minor is unsurpassed in legally protecting a child outside of their parent's care until the age of eighteen. This allows decisions to be made in the best interest of the child. It protects the grandparent and child's rights without removing parental rights from the biological parents. In fact, in many states it's referred to "temporary" because the biological parents can apply to reclaim their children as long as they prove they are fit and able to assume all parental responsibilities in front of a judge.

Lynne's Story

Our daughter was no longer living in our home and was using meth every day. We knew we needed some kind of written document to protect our grandson, whom we were now in charge of raising. As grandparents, we discovered we had no real legal rights. If something happened to our addict daughter, the Department of Social Services could easily take our grandson from us and place him in a foster home. We weren't willing to take a chance on that happening so I went on an Internet search looking for answers. I found a document called Durable Power of Attorney for a Minor. With that form, it appeared I could get him medical attention without a hassle. So I printed it out and approached my daughter for a signature. She readily signed it, but not before questioning me to make sure I wasn't taking her child away.

About a year later, to my dismay, I discovered the State of California didn't recognize that particular form at hospitals or if I wanted to register my grandson for school. I was informed we needed temporary legal guardianship in place. I wasn't looking forward to approaching her to sign *that* one.

Meanwhile, our daughter was quickly spiraling down into her drug use. She wasn't thinking straight and I became petrified she'd sneak into our home and take her son in the middle of the night. If she did, there was nothing we could do. This was even more of a motivator to get the proper documents in place to protect him— and us—in case that ever happened. I was told even if the biological parent was clearly under the influence and wanted to take the child; we had no recourse. Because she was the legal parent, the police wouldn't stop her. This prompted me to get the ball rolling.

We found a lawyer and retained him to draw up a Petition for Temporary Letters of Guardianship. With papers in hand, we immediately called our daughter to arrange a meeting. We explained to her it wasn't possible to get him medical treatment in case of an emergency unless we had these papers. Still, she accused us of trying to take her child away from her. She wouldn't budge even when we tried to convince her it was in her son's best interest. She only began to soften when my husband asked, "What if you can't be found and your son needs serious medical help?" As soon as he added she could always go to court and petition to get him back, she agreed to sign. To make sure she wouldn't back out, our eldest daughter presented the papers to her for signing. We knew she'd never refuse her sister.

Our court date was scheduled within thirty days and, before a judge, we were granted guardianship. Protected in the best way possible, we finally had rights and could make decisions in the best interest of our grandson, get him medical attention if needed, sign him up for sports and register him for school. At last, we could relax and my fears and nightmares of him being taken while we slept, ceased.

I wished there was a similar document that could also be signed to quiet the fears I had about my daughter, her safety and even her life. But at least her son was protected. At least we were able to do that much.

KINSHIP SOLDIER

Kinship foster care is a good choice if the grandparents believe strongly in the likelihood of reunification with the birth parents. Research from the Southern Area Consortium of Human Services at San Diego State University, California, found kinship caregiver's close ties to the child and the child's birth family inherently support family bonds. It can also provide continuity, lessen separation trauma, preserve family ties and offer growth and development.

Similar to guardianship, the requirements vary from state to state. Like foster care, kinship care offers monetary compensation, making it appealing. However, compared to traditional foster care, kinship is fairly new and many wrinkles have not been ironed out. The program remains inconsistent from state to state, with kinship foster parents receiving less financial support, fewer services and less contact with child welfare workers than traditional foster care parents.

Cathy's Story

Because of my husband's income and limited resources, we looked into becoming licensed foster parents. With four grandchildren to raise, we needed all the help we could get. Kinship foster care was the option we chose and was a whole new ballgame. I recently heard from the owner of our foster care agency most agencies wouldn't deal with kinship care because it is so different from traditional foster care. In kinship, we not only have emotional ties to the children but also to their parents. In addition and sometimes not favorably, we have to deal with the drama of extended family members, which often causes complications.

Some of our family members didn't understand why they had to play by the same rules as we did. Even though they weren't the individuals asking to be foster parents, they still needed to fulfill certain requirements simply because they were related to the children. Like us, they had to have background checks, FBI finger printing, CPR Certification and First Aid classes.

So while we were going through our own stress of getting everything in order, we also had to listen to their ongoing gripes about what they were asked to complete. We just hoped they would settle down and do the work. Luckily, they did and we became kinship foster parents. The payments we receive as foster parents are helping us with the children's expenses.

Soon, we hope to apply for Permanent Managing Conservatorship, which is the name given to guardianship in Texas. Along with our kinship care, we hope this will be a good marriage in supporting and caring for our new family. Since I don't know what the future holds, I believe this was the right choice for our family.

FOSTER TACTIC

In the face of overwhelming odds, there are times when foster care turns out to be the best option for everyone. Sometimes grandparents just can't do it all—and ultimately it's all about what's best for the child.

Renea's Story

Twenty-six years ago, before my daughter was born, I was told I wouldn't be able to have children. Needless to say, her birth was my greatest gift. But my beautiful daughter became an addict when she was twelve years old and methamphetamine was her drug of choice. While addicted, she also became pregnant and over the years, gave birth to four children. Her choices made her unfit, as well as unable to care for her kids.

Consequently, I found myself with no choice but to stand in her place. Suddenly and unexpectedly, I was a forty-six-year-old single parent to her four children. These babies had already been through so much.

For most of the children's lives, I'd allowed them, including my daughter, to live with me. Even though my daughter used drugs, she was still trying to be a wonderful mother. She always dressed the children nicely, bathed them, fed them and took them to all their appointments. The children's father however, also an addict, was another story. He fought with my daughter, and would often leave the children in unsafe places around unsafe people. He even robbed me several times, while I was the one providing for all of them.

I knew it wasn't a good thing for my grandkids to have an addicted mother and father but there wasn't anything I could do. I tried many times to legally get someone's attention and help me intervene on behalf of the children. But because my daughter appeared to be a responsible mother, I got nowhere. It wasn't until somebody at my grandson's preschool noticed something wasn't right and submitted a complaint, that the Department of Children and Family finally paid attention. The kids were immediately put into foster care.

The children's dad ended up in prison and my daughter, though given numerous chances to clean up her life by the court, without her children; plummeted further and further into her addiction. She tried rehab but was unsuccessful and was also placed in jail on drug-related charges. The twins were two and one-half years old when my daughter relinquished her parental rights.

More than anything, I wanted to keep all the children with me but couldn't because I was injured at work and had to have extensive surgery on my shoulder. The twins were only six months old at the time, and it would have been impossible for me to hold them, let alone care for their needs. Due to my circumstances, as much as I wanted to take care of all four grandchildren, I was worried I couldn't give them everything they deserved. I lived in a small house, drove a small car and had a small bank account. I also had emphysema, severe bronchitis and was a smoker. These smart, amazing, beautiful children deserved more. I wanted them but was not sure it was good for them or good for me. And so I made a painful decision to compromise. The two older children had never shared the same foster home as the younger twins and I decided I would try to adopt the oldest two. I also fought to become an interested party so I could visit the twins. Luckily, I received my own regularly scheduled visits.

Because I was going to fight to be in the kids' lives, I had to distance myself from my daughter. It was heartbreaking for me to watch addiction steal my only child—a child who, ironically, I should never have been able to have. I mourned her often. She was my best friend. But the love for my grandchildren, who were so innocent and stole my heart at birth, sent me into a soul-searching, heart-wrenching dilemma as I struggled to try and fit the pieces together so that everyone could benefit as much as possible.

It was such a blessing to know the twins' foster mom adored them so much and was planning to adopt them. I was also grateful she had accepted me, and their siblings as extended family, and we would be allowed to remain in their lives. They lived almost thirty miles away and because of scheduling conflicts, I could only get there monthly, but I did this as often as I could.

As of today, I am still working. My job with developmentally disabled adults has been very demanding. In addition, my oldest six-year-old grandson, who was especially hit hard by his mother's addiction, has a combination of Oppositional Defiance Disorder and Attention Deficit Hyperactivity Disorder, while my granddaughter is developing her own set of challenging behaviors that often need to be addressed. Some days I'm at my wit's end and am so tired I can hardly breathe.

Still, I love my grandchildren with every ounce of my being. The oldest two are with me as a kinship placement and I am waiting for final approval to adopt them. Unfortunately, I qualify for no additional help and the daily struggle is real. Both the kids miss their parents greatly with many questions and tears, mainly about their mommy. I do my best to give comfort, love, and understanding for what they have been through and the adjustments they are still experiencing. I try to answer questions as best I can and would love, more than anything, to take their pain away. They have been through way too much.

I pray our adoption is final soon so we can attempt to find closure and continue to build our lives with love and happiness. I feel blessed I am being given another chance at being a better parent by the gift of these children in my life.

ADOPTION WARRIOR

The most definitive form of permanent protection and stability for a grandchild is adoption. Of course, this is not always the optimum choice if there is a chance for the biological parent or parents to assume their parental role again in the future. But if this prospect looks dim and a grandparent wants to take complete and permanent responsibility for the child, eliminating the possibility the child's birth parents will be able legally to interfere; then adoption could be the best choice.

Adoption benefits include the choice to legally name a guardian for the child, an important advantage in the event something unforeseen should happen to the grandparent. In the event that does happen, the adopted child will also automatically receive the grandparent's Social Security benefits until the age of eighteen. The most surprising detail of adoption is receiving a new birth certificate naming the grandparents as the birth parents. But above all, the advantage of adoption is giving the child a secure and permanent place in the family.

Lynne's Story

Six-year-old Brady was so excited about the prospect he was going to be adopted, he told everyone at school he already *was*. It was like the cherry on top of a sundae—adoption was his security, giving him permanent a place in the scheme of things. Sure, he'd called us Mom and Dad since he was a toddler and we had legal guardianship. Still, there was something permanent and stabilizing about adoption.

We spoke to a family lawyer and began the process. Our lawyer said adoption was slow, tedious and could take almost a year to be finalized. In addition, it was expensive. We had to pay a large fee to our lawyer and also to the Department of Social Services. The paperwork itself was intimidating enough to call the whole thing off. The forms stacked up to over an inch in thickness, very detailed and repetitive. Stu and I were investigated and questioned about everything we'd done in our lives—even about our first sexual encounter. Who can remember that?

A diligent search for the alleged birth father was conducted, though it was done several years before when we applied for legal guardianship. Although he wasn't on the birth certificate, no actual proof he was the father and he hadn't seen Brady since birth; he still had the right of notice. Once he received this notice, he had thirty days to respond or lose his parental rights. This alone scared me. With his being older and possibly more mature, I was concerned he could have had a change of heart and might contest the adoption.

As soon as the paperwork was completed, Stu, Brady and I were scheduled to meet with a social worker from the Department of Social Services. I was anxious about being questioned and how I'd be perceived. But all my nerves were put to rest once we met her. She was approachable and relaxed, which made for a more conversational meeting, rather than the nerve-racking questioning I was expecting. She briefly met with Brady, seemingly to determine how well adjusted he was and if he was happy with us.

Afterwards, Brady went back to the waiting room, where our son, Josh, stayed with him while Stu and I finished the interview. Then the social worker said she had some news for us. She said that, to date, Brady's alleged birth father had not been found. We were relieved to say the least.

After our paperwork was accepted, we got a court date. As informed, the entire adoption process had taken close to a year to complete, and was to culminate before a judge.

We were just a week away from the ceremony when we described to our inquisitive Brady how we thought the day would transpire. He told us he was so happy we were going to be his mom and dad "for real."

"Now, I'll have the brothers and sister I always wanted!" he said, which really threw me. I knew what he was referring to but couldn't believe he got the concept.

"How so?" I asked, wanting to make sure this six-year-old meant what I thought he meant.

"Well, Mom, it's like this," he straightforwardly said. "My aunt and two uncles are your children, too, so they'll become my sister and brothers."

He got it. Even my older kids didn't get it when I first told them.

"Brady," I said, as I kissed him on the forehead, "you never cease to amaze me."

"Oh, and one more thing," he excitedly said. "I can't wait to see my cousins' faces when they have to call me uncle. Now, when can we see the judge?"

IT'S OFFICIAL

Joy's Story

I t was official. We had our adoption finalization Monday. It was an emotional day and the end of fifteen months of jumping through hoops, inspections, visits with social workers, filling out paperwork and too many more details to recall. All the while, we watched my daughter and son-in-law self-destruct. They relapsed repeatedly, did jail time, lived out of cars and finally separated for good.

Today, they see their child about once every three or four weeks. And that is fine with me. We are focused on our grandson. He is the light of our lives, and though I so wish I could have just been a grandma; I am instead a recycled mom.

It hit me again when I took him to the pediatrician on Wednesday. For the first time, with the encouragement of the staff members, who could not stop congratulating me on the adoption, I signed the "relationship to patient" portion of his medical form as "mother." I cried.

III

COLLATERAL DAMAGE

"Show me a hero and I will write you a tragedy."

—*F. Scott Fitzgerald*

UNDER ATTACK

It's important to remember, even though the children we've taken into our homes are in a better place, it's not a place they chose. Many children feel the emptiness of their bio parents not being present. We try our best to provide loving homes, but nonetheless, we feel the pressure and the children feel the void.

If the bio parent is currently in and out of our grandchildren's lives, there are questions as to why their natural parents aren't the ones caring for them. If the addict parent is deceased, those questions remain and the child still wants to know why.

Many of us have explained the bio parent story in an age-appropriate manner and in a loving way so the children won't feel their parents are bad, which could reflect negatively on the child's feeling of self-worth or even cause them to blame themselves. Still, not being with their bio parents can cause behavioral issues. Poor behavior and eruptions are common. Therapists say a child will usually act out where he or she feels safe. We are their refuge. Our job is to absorb the shock and even be the brunt of the outbursts until they hopefully dissipate. Until that time, many grandparents have to deal with this reality every single day.

Cathy's Story

It's been almost two years since the kids were placed in our care. Raising four kids has been a definite challenge. We knew our lives would be different but never expected to be so surprised by some of their behavior.

The children came to us confused, angry, and because we were the closest to them, often lashed out in attack yelling, "I hate you!" They were innocent victims and still didn't understand why they couldn't live with their own mommy and daddy. Even if a child's mom and dad lived on the street or in a drug house in horrid conditions, I don't think it would matter to the child. The bond is that strong.

Some days I just wanted to throw in the towel and walk away because sometimes it was more than I felt I could handle. Instead of being disciplinarian and caretaker, I wished I could have been just the grandma and do the "fun stuff" with them, like the other grandma. But I couldn't. They needed parents and we were it. Of course, we would gladly have given up our parenting roles if my son and daughter-in-law could have been whole again, but that was not in our power.

Still, I am in constant upheaval, one day mourning for my son who is still alive and other days holding onto the faith in my son's ability to become whatever he wants to be. I will continue to hope for his recovery, knowing he may not make it. Even so, I will never give up on him. I pray he can find himself, again, and beat this disease.

Meanwhile, we will do what it takes to be here and give our grandkids stable lives; no matter how they behave or how long it takes. I know they love us, as we love them. We can only hope time will help them heal, and their anger and confusion will diminish the longer they're with us.

ANGRY YOUNG SOLDIER

Jackie's Story

When I was thirty-six, I took my youngest son to register for preschool. As I gazed at the other moms in the room, I noticed they all looked at least ten years younger and I found myself wondering, what I was doing with a four-year-old. That was twenty-seven years ago. In a few months I'll be sixty-three. At a time when I thought all of my children would be leading happy and successful lives of their own, I am unexpectedly raising another child. He is now eight and I again find myself wondering; what I am doing with an eight-year-old.

All four of my children have struggled with mental health issues and addiction in some form or another—alcohol, pills, cocaine, and heroin. My oldest daughter, whose son is in my care, has been in and out of hospitals, jail and rehab for over twenty years. There are many days when I don't think I will make it, but I'm still here. After all, I am responsible. I am all he has. He depends on me.

The first year with my grandson was the most difficult. There were many changes taking place for all of us. I barely knew this child. In a way, purely out of self-preservation, I was determined to not know him and to not love him. I had gone through too much hurt when his older siblings were with us intermittently over most of the years of their lives. However, I was left with no choice with this one. His dad dropped him off with us and disappeared. At the time, no one knew where his mom, my daughter, was.

The next thing I knew, the Department of Social Services (DSS) was involved. My husband and I were asked if we'd be willing to let him remain with us temporarily. We were told it would be about six to nine months. His parents had to go to rehab, attend drug classes and parenting classes. For a while, things looked good and they complied. Because they were doing everything they had to do, they were given three to four days of weekly visits to spend time with their son, at our discretion. But these visits were not pleasant. They were fraught with angry barbs towards anyone they could blame for their situation. They took no responsibility for their actions and everything was the fault of the government, DSS or anyone else even remotely involved.

Unfortunately, our grandson picked up on all of this and became a very angry child. Angry children are difficult to deal with because they don't know how to process their anger and resentment. They don't even really understand why they are angry. He alternately talked back, acted out, cried, pouted and retreated in silence. He couldn't or wouldn't tell us how he felt or why he did the things he did. Hoping he would calm down, we kept telling him the situation wouldn't last. We told ourselves it was temporary. A person can live through anything if they know it's temporary. Right?

As the months stretched into a year and then longer, things did not get better. We talked about giving up and letting them put him in foster care. Actually, my husband talked about it while I cried and refused to consider it. It took a huge toll on our relationship.

We couldn't agree on anything. I felt my husband was too harsh in his discipline and he felt I was too lenient. Unfortunately, we both had a tendency to take our frustrations out on each other and even more regrettably, on our grandson. It was a very difficult time for us.

Almost two years later, the court gave us legal permanent custody. The only way his parents could get him back would have been to complete a treatment plan, hire a lawyer and take us to court. I didn't see that happening. It was heartbreaking and frustrating to know they could have done it. They could have had their son back if they had just tried—if they had just completed the plan. It wasn't a difficult plan. I will probably never understand why they didn't. In fact, they still could. That door is still open. It would just take a little effort on their part—a little effort and focus that neither of them seems to have.

Little by little, over time our grandson has come around and his anger has lifted. I think he finally realized he has had a good life with us. It has been a place of routine and stability. He even made the honor roll at school and seems so much happier. We have settled into a comfortable schedule. There are still rough days. There are days when he wants to see his parents and can't. But, at least, he no longer pouts or cries. He seems resigned to make the best of each day and most of the time just focuses on being a kid.

We still feel we are too old to be parenting, again. Sometimes I miss the quiet times and being able to watch a TV program or do something I want to do without interruption. I am not a fan of getting a young child ready for school every morning, making lunches, monitoring homework or trying to fit in teacher conferences, doctor appointments and even haircuts into my daily routine. These aren't activities I would have chosen at this time in my life.

But the indisputable reality is this child we never asked to be in our lives, who has brought us a lot of disruption, has also brought us much joy and laughter. We are blessed he is with us; and he is blessed to have received a second chance. I can't imagine life without him now and that makes all the changes and disruption more than worth it.

AWOL

A soldier that leaves his post without permission is said to have gone AWOL (Absent Without Leave). That's exactly what many addict parents have done to their children. Feelings of neglect are rampant with these children, which we feel, too. Our adult children are placing us in the position of assuming their parental responsibility and we, quite understandably, resent them for it. Seeing our grandchildren deal with disappointment breaks our hearts especially when this is often due to the addict parents making promises they can't or won't keep.

LarLei's Story

It was autumn and I could feel change was in the air. I craved it and looked for it. Every morning I'd go to my favorite advice website. I felt it helped me grow wiser by gathering strength, taking the lead, listening, surrendering and waiting. Once I was even advised to clean my house. I thought maybe that could mean we would move soon. I certainly wasn't expecting it could mean I, and my sixty-year-old childless husband, were to become instant parents to a seven-year-old.

Five hundred miles away, my son's story was filled with the typical addict details. His history of drug abuse began at just thirteen years old when we received a call from the ER informing us he had overdosed on a variety of over-the-counter drugs. I knew then we were in for a wild ride but couldn't begin to imagine just how wild. I remember prophetically thinking I better buckle my seat belt.

In classic addict fashion, our son had everything and lost it. We spent years listening to all his excuses as well as the bizarre stories and elaborate schemes he created, while he frequently asked for money.

That previous spring, he and his children were homeless.My two grandkids were nine and six, and though the other grandparents that were nearby were limited; it seemed that they were the ones who housed and fed the grandkids and got them to school. My grandson would often call me from their house while his parents wandered in and out. Sometimes he'd call saying they were in a motel room.

At the end of that summer, my grandson came to Florida for a visit with us.An aunt drove him down from Tennessee, but my six-year-old granddaughter was too young to come, so she stayed with her other grandparents.Meanwhile, my son reported they were looking for a house to rent. During each evening phone call to his parents, my grandson would ask them if they'd found a house, if they'd bought a car or if they'd gotten a job. During that visit, as we watched him interact by telephone with them, we learned things that disturbed us. I had already figured out my son was back on drugs, but I never thought my daughter-in-law would also be addicted. But she was.

After my grandson returned to Tennessee and started back to school, he would call me on the phone every evening from the other grandparent's house just to talk. His parents still didn't have transportation or a home. Then without notice, the Tennessee grandparents moved across town and the phone calls abruptly ceased. Their number was out of service and they didn't own cell phones. Very concerned, I left messages for my son and his girl-friend, but they didn't return my texts or voice messages. Finally, I called the elementary school where both grandkids were enrolled and spoke to the school resource officer. Abuse and neglect was suspected. He called the Department of Child Services (DCS).

My ex-husband (my son's father), his wife and their eleven-year-old daughter lived in a neighboring county. They'd also kept our grandson during part of his summer vacation and they too, were disturbed and concerned. At the beginning of October they met with my husband and me and we all agreed we had no choice but to file for custody of the two grandkids. It was decided they would live with my ex-husband and his family so we didn't have to split up the siblings.

We filed for custody just in the nick of time as we learned that DCS was already planning to either place them with fos-ter parents or with the other grandparents, who we did not feel were a healthy option for the children. So my ex-husband and I each drove eight hours to Tennessee for the emergency custody hearing. The courtroom was packed. I watched and listened to cases just like ours. Grandparents answered the judge's questions and testified against their own children in an effort to keep their grandkids safe. Mothers pleaded with the judge to get their kids back, crying because they hadn't held their children in months and promising too late to do a better job parenting. Then it was our turn.

The other grandparents were also trying to get custody of the children. The children's parents weren't there. However, just as our attorney was presenting our petition, the children's parents staggered into the courtroom. They were reeking of meth. The judge sat up straight, looked at them and without more questions, signed over emergency custody of our almost seven-year-old granddaughter and nine-year-old grandson to my ex-husband and me. The hearing was then reset for ninety days with orders for the parents to get a hair follicle drug test.

My granddaughter had seen me less than ten times in her seven-year-old life, including the moment she was born. She'd seen her step-grandpa only about twice. However, the minute the DCS transitioned her to us, she held tightly to my hand and hasn't let go since.

After court on that October day, the children's parents and the other grandparents were calm and cooperative. We all agreed to meet at the local park to say goodbye and to celebrate my granddaughter's seventh birthday, which was the very next day.

My granddaughter, still tightly holding my hand, led me around Walmart, while we shopped for her party. Then at the park, she was zigzagging me all around the playground, while I played with her. Even though her other grandparents, her parents, an assortment of aunts, uncles, and cousins were all there; no one else ventured out onto the playground with us to participate—not even her parents.

Then the agreement for the kids to live with my ex-husband unexpectedly and suddenly changed. His wife explained she just couldn't handle two children in addition to her own, and wanted to only take the boy. My childless husband had already said he couldn't either. But when I called him and told him the judge gave us custody and he asked, "Are you telling me to get the guest room ready for a seven-year-old girl?"—I knew he was ready.

"Yes," I answered.

At that moment I knew we'd all be fine. He was ready. And in a strange way, so was I.

DESERTION

It's hard to comprehend the heartache some of our grandchildren have had to deal with at such young ages. As grandparents, we just want to make everything okay for these innocent survivors and hope they can grow up healthy beyond being drug-exposed, beyond living through parental abuse and beyond experiencing abandonment.

Pattee's Story

My daughter started using drugs at fourteen and was already addicted to methamphetamine and other drugs when she became pregnant at nineteen. Homeless and on the streets, after six months, she was willing to go to counseling—anything—just to come home. She said she stopped using about three months into her pregnancy and though drug-free at delivery, was still only six months clean. This gave me great concern about the potential impact on the baby, as well my daughter's sobriety. I knew it takes about eighteen months clean from methamphetamine before the brain is as healed as it is going to be from the meth damage.

And then I heard it. That cry. Our granddaughter was born with that strange wailing shrill cry I knew was characteristic of a drug-exposed baby. She also exhibited extreme anxiety. Oh, my heart. I wondered if her early exposure to the drugs could have caused it. I held this helpless infant firmly and took extra care to soothe her. I also managed to convince the head nurse to allow me to stay all night so I could rock the baby to calm her frequent shaking and trembling.

In the hospital, my daughter was too tired to tend to her infant, and her boyfriend (not the baby's father) was not present for the birth. So of course, I ended up as the one to initially bond with the baby. I encouraged my daughter to hold her baby but she was barely interested. At home, she was still very tired and slept a lot. When the baby awoke at night, I would feed her and then carry her to the living room where we'd listen to classical music and sleep on the couch, allowing the new mother to rest. And so, the baby and I bonded further.

Eventually, mother and baby moved out but I saw them daily. When my precious granddaughter began to walk and talk, she would run towards me, embrace me and would excitedly call out, "Grandma!" Many times, she would want me to stay with her while she fell asleep in her crib. I would lie on the floor and hold her hand. She still seemed full of anxiety. As a toddler, she was fearful, especially at night. I wasn't sure if that was just more anxiety or because of the constant fighting going on in the house between her mother and boyfriend. They made it a habit to call the police on each other regularly.

My granddaughter often wanted to stay with me so I would have her come for sleepovers, especially when her mother broke up with her boyfriend. Not knowing her biological father, my granddaughter saw him as her daddy, and at three years old she lost him—the only daddy she ever knew and loved. We tried to buffer her loss but I don't think she ever got over it.

Unexpected Heroes

Now at ten years old, she feels bereft and different without a known bio father and having been rejected by the daddy who had once adored her. This same man had once assured me he would never deny her, even if he and my daughter split up. But now, even during rare exchanges, he barely acknowledges my granddaughter. Because of this, she avoids contact and prefers to ignore him. Still, if he were to attempt to rekindle a relationship with her, I'm sure she would happily respond.

For awhile, my daughter had stabilized and worked hard to stay clean while very busy with two jobs, school, a new boyfriend and the birth of two more children. But when our granddaughter was seven years old, unawares to us, my daughter began dabbling again in drugs. By the time she was eight, my daughter's addiction had escalated as she moved on to oxies, crack and ultimately heroin. At the height of her addiction, my granddaughter became the victim of her mother's poor treatment of her. My daughter would ignore her daughter, but fawn over her two young sons. When we saw how miserable our granddaughter was, I sat down with all three grandchildren and asked them what was going on. I was so upset to discover my daughter had become abusive to her daughter, screaming at her, slapping her and throwing her down on her bed. I was beside myself. But I knew I was powerless to really help because they were her children, not mine.

It wasn't always like that. For several years, my daughter was an attentive mother, taking care of her responsibilities. It was heartbreaking to see her emotionally abandon her children. Gratefully, she began to allow us to keep the kids longer and longer, first by asking us and eventually, by not returning to collect them when she said she would. We soon kept the children six nights a week.

Especially upsetting for my granddaughter was when her mother would make contact. She would only request to speak to the boys and my granddaughter did not miss these slights. Her mother would only call to talk to her if she wanted information or to guilt-trip her or accuse her of loving me more than her. My daughter finally abdicated all parenting, which was classified as abandonment and we were able to obtain guardianship.

For Mother's Day, my granddaughter's teacher had each child make a gift, which included a game. My granddaughter chose to give me the gift. The game asked the question, "If you could have one wish…" My granddaughter's wish was to live with her mother, again. Tragically, after everything she had been through, after all of the accusations, hurt and rejection, this little girl still loved and missed her mother. I asked her, "If your mother got a place to live tomorrow, would you go with her?" Her sad, yet honest answer was, "No. I just wish it was like it used to be."

I know our granddaughter loves us, relies on us and is mostly happy. But she often feels lonely and confused as to why her life turned out the way it has. She is a loving, kind, sweet-natured child who is also attractive, bright, hardworking and responsible. Yet her mother's legacy to her is one of uncertainty, with understandable concerns about her worthiness. She is such an amazing young girl but unfortunately, was negatively impacted from the moment of conception.

Watching my granddaughter, I can clearly see abandonment by a parent has a lasting impact on a child, no matter how much the child is loved by others. We have done our best to love and guide her, but wonder if it will be enough to help her be confident and make good choices as she reaches adolescence and adulthood. We wonder if it will be enough to give her the foundation she must have to live the kind of successful and productive life her mother couldn't. We can only hope what we have done will be enough. We are committed to doing it as long as we are able.

POST-TRAUMATIC STRESS

Our addicted children's children have experienced more trauma than the average child. And tragically, too many have already been through hell and back by being exposed to drugs before birth, having to endure the aftermath of withdrawal and/or residual concerns like Attention Deficit Hyperactivity Disorder, Obsessive Compulsive Disorder, Oppositional Defiant Disorder, learning differences and even food and sensory issues.

Some of our grandchildren have been around drug paraphernalia in drug houses with their own parent or parents using drugs right in front of them. Others have witnessed violence, sex or been the victim of physical, mental and/or sexual abuse. And just as dreadful, some of our young children have even experienced living on the streets with addict parents and showed obvious signs of neglect—a result of circumstances most of us can't even imagine.

Fortunately, many of our grandchildren were lucky enough to escape those traumatic experiences because they were fortunate to have lived with us either from the beginning or soon after when their parents couldn't or wouldn't care for them. Yet we discovered they still showed signs of abandonment and other issues due to the addict parent who was not available emotionally to them, or had physically left.

Not surprisingly, these children frequently experience Post Traumatic Stress Disorder or PTSD. The behaviors from this disorder vary greatly in type and intensity from child to child and may include anger, anxiety, night terrors and fear of being alone, of the dark or of dying.

Lynne's Story

We could never understand why Brady was always so fearful. He was afraid of the dark, afraid of monsters in the closet, afraid to be alone and mostly afraid we were going to die. Since our daughter's death, he has carried the fear we'll also die too soon and makes us promise often that we will try to stay alive for as long as we can.

Brady has always lived with us. Along with our daughter, we were a three-parent family, until she returned to the world of drugs. He was a little over two years old when we asked her to leave our home to find sobriety. The night she left for sober living, he screamed and cried bitterly. Understandably, it devastated him and the separation took its toll. We didn't realize it at the time but he had developed a mild case of Post Traumatic Stress Disorder. He was trying to adjust to everything he was experiencing in his little head, but didn't know how to cope with all those feelings.

As much as we loved him, took him to play therapy and gave him a stable home—it made no difference—his fears and anxiety remained. When he was three, he randomly kicked, hit and spit at us in a fit of rage. Then he stopped, said he was sorry, told us he loved us and said he didn't know what came over him. We were told children are most likely to act out where they feel comfortable but it certainly wasn't comfortable for us.

Thankfully, time seemed to help. His anger slowly dissipated, the longer we were his sole parents. However, his fears, though less intense, stayed. They were more apparent at bedtime and he would beg one us to lay down with him while he fell asleep, saying he was afraid. We'd leave afterwards, but he would wake up almost every night yelling for us at three o'clock in the morning. In order to avoid interrupted sleep, one of us would sleep with him through the night. This went on for more years than expected or wanted.

When Brady was five years old, he agreed to try to sleep alone, which we attempted to do gradually. It worked for a while but his fears returned and he again pleaded with one of us to stay, saying he'd sleep by himself when he was six. When he turned six, he said seven. He is now eleven. He still likes one of us to lay with him until he falls asleep but now he's able to sleep alone until morning most days. It's a process.

Last summer when he was just ten, his friends were going to overnight camp. We knew this would be quite a challenge, especially for him. Still, we asked him if he also wanted to go. He surprised us by saying he'd like to try it. Even though we described what it would be like and he just might be homesick for a few days or longer; he insisted he could do it. Since he was a very social kid and made friends easily and, especially because there would be other kids in the bunk, we agreed he'd probably be fine. Well, he wasn't and it was a disaster. He missed us so much that it was completely overwhelming for him. He cried under his blanket each night and sent postcards to us with "Help" all over them. As soon as we received the first postcard, we called the camp and said we'd come get him that night. But Brady got on the phone and told us he'd tough it out because there was another boy more upset than he was. He didn't want to leave him alone.

When we picked him up on his last day of camp, he ran to us and said he made the biggest mistake of his life in deciding to go to overnight camp. He said he missed us so much he couldn't find joy in anything and told us he was devastated for life. Just the fact he finished his two weeks at camp, was able to verbalize his feelings and take responsibility for his decision, was huge to us. We knew he was maturing and thought maybe this experience would be a turning point for him. Perhaps he'd surprise us and sleep alone at home? Nope. No such luck.

Although we're seeing small steps of improvement in his anxiety level and fears, he still wants me to lay down with him at bedtime. His therapist once said he would let go when he was able. We're okay with that but also don't want to enable him and stunt his growth and independence. So we are now initiating our plan to slowly have him sleep on his own. He said okay. It seems to be working.

CASUALTIES OF WAR

Witnessing a drug addicted newborn go through the pain of withdrawal is horrific and not easy to forget. Adult drug addicts at least have an understanding of the physical consequences of withdrawal—but newborns? How can a newborn be soothed and made whole, again? Drug babies are usually underweight, unable to regulate body temperatures, hypersensitive to touch, do not sleep well and are generally extremely uncomfortable while the drugs leave their systems. They cry, they sweat, they startle easily, they have diarrhea, can't keep food down, they have body tremors and often have respiratory issues. And those are just the physical symptoms.

Many doctors recommend methadone treatment. Although milder, this is somewhat controversial as it is replacing one drug for another. Some grandparents who have custody of drug babies have refused drug therapy and opted for alternative holistic treatment. The infants are put on a strict schedule for bathing, napping and feeding followed by a soothing massage and warm bath. Swaddling is also used so the infants will feel safe and secure. These babies are held close, rocked and sung to softly. Sometimes classical music is played when they become highly irritable. Even special care nurses in hospital nurseries use swings, quiet rooms and "cuddlers" who sit and rock these babies. These "difficult-to-calm" babies need constant soothing and don't sleep for long periods of time, unlike babies without these issues. Horribly, withdrawal can last for the first five or six months of the baby's life. And, unfortunately, a high percentage of drug babies go on to experience the residual effects of drug exposure as young children through behavioral and learning disorders.

Bonnie's Story

Instead of the usual joy we should have felt when my husband and I learned we were going to be first-time grandparents, we were in utter shock. There was no way this could be true. The week before receiving this news, I had taken my daughter to my obstetrician, who did a pelvic exam and renewed her birth control pills. I trusted this doctor implicitly, since he was the one who delivered my daughter twenty-three years ago and I was still seeing him. How could he have missed this?

Five days after her doctor appointment, my husband and I made the ninety-minute drive to take my daughter to a detox facility when I got the call from her. She told me I had to come pick her up because she was pregnant and they could not give her the detox meds. She added she knew I wouldn't believe her so she handed the phone to a nurse who confirmed the news.

After picking her up, my daughter and I returned to my obstetrician the next day and confirmed she was indeed pregnant. But even more shocking was the ultrasound estimated she was five and a half months along. At first, my daughter gasped and then cried when the ultrasound technician moved the wand over her stomach and a baby's image appeared on the monitor. She asked if we wanted to know the gender and we discovered it was a little girl.

We were referred to a neonatologist. Interestingly, not because of concerns about the heroin and other drugs my daughter had been using, but because she had taken birth control pills somewhat consistently throughout the pregnancy. The doctor said it was a miracle she became pregnant.

In the womb, the baby appeared to be completely normal. We were informed my daughter would need to begin daily methadone treatment so she did not spontaneously abort. They identified a provider in Indiana, even though we lived in Northern Kentucky. So the next morning, we made the drive, and our daughter began a daily regimen of methadone. She continued to take the minimum dosage until the baby's birth.

My husband and I paid the doctor's fee plus the fifteen dollars a day for the methadone. It was a small price to pay, we felt, for the safety of our granddaughter and the least we could do to give this new baby a fighting chance. It paid off because our daughter delivered a healthy seven pound, six ounce beautiful baby girl by C-Section that December. Our daughter also agreed to allow us to be limited guardians for the child so she could be added to my husband's health insurance. While the baby was still in the Neonatal Intensive Care Unit (NICU), my husband and I raced to the courthouse.

When we returned to the hospital, we were strongly cautioned there was a possibility our granddaughter could have developmental delays, but we wouldn't know until she began to grow and mature. Unfortunately, we had more immediate concerns. The baby had begun experiencing withdrawal symptoms from methadone. As if we didn't have enough worries, a caseworker from Children's Protective Services (CPS) visited us while my daughter was still in the hospital. She told us they were planning to open a case against her in Ohio where the baby had been born. Why? Not because my daughter or her baby tested positive for any other drug but because the baby tested positive for methadone. I argued it had been prescribed to allow the pregnancy to safely continue. As soon as the obstetrician intervened at my request, the charges were dropped. My doctor reassured the caseworker a plan was in place for the baby to go home with mom and grandparents. He added he was certain the grandmother would not let anything happen to the baby. He was absolutely right.

I was so proud my daughter voluntarily disclosed all the information about her first five and one-half months of drug use during her pregnancy to the medical staff. Without it, she and the baby might have been discharged from the hospital before withdrawal symptoms showed up and were treated. Still, along with her guilt about her drug use, my daughter felt stigmatized by many of the medical personnel she encountered. It gave me a new perspective regarding why a new mother might try to hide her drug history from medical providers—but not my daughter. She even insisted she be drug-tested to prove she was not taking anything besides the methadone. With this information, the medical staff was on high alert the baby would possibly be in withdrawal so they could intervene and help at the earliest signs.

The baby spent fifteen days in the NICU tapering down from the methadone. This necessary medication to avoid a spontaneous abortion and save the baby's life caused the baby to endure the ill effects of it. It was so painful to watch an innocent newborn suffer the consequences of her mom's addiction. I made a promise to her I would do whatever I could in the future to protect her from the effects of her parents' disease. I wanted so badly to hold her, to rock her, to just love on her. But the nurses said babies withdrawing from methadone were extremely sensitive to touch, and physical contact with her was limited to feeding and changing times. I made sure we were there for every one of them.

My granddaughter was finally discharged from the hospital and I held onto my hopes for both my daughter and granddaughter that things were going to be okay. I was so naive. I didn't understand the magnitude of my daughter's disease. While we had no real proof our daughter was using again, red flags were going up. She seemed disinterested in caring for her newborn. At first we thought it might be severe post-partum depression, so we had her agree to enter the psych ward at the same hospital where she had delivered eight weeks earlier. After she was admitted, we sadly learned she wasn't done with her drugs. She tested positive for opiates and other illegal substances.

We also found out that instead of attending the college classes she began after the baby's birth (which we paid for while also watching the baby), she had sold her textbooks and spent the six hours of school time each day out of the house doing drugs. As soon as she threatened she was going to remove the baby from our home because we would not give her money and keys to a car, we applied for emergency temporary custody.

This happened on a Friday and we were initially denied. So we asked for a hearing in front of a judge for the following Monday. We were concerned having the added weekend days without custody because our daughter might try to take the baby. Consequently, my husband and I decided the best thing to prevent her from taking the baby was say the judge had stated the baby could not be removed from our home until the case was heard. We weren't sure she would believe us but it worked.

At the hearing on Monday, emergency temporary custody was granted. Our daughter was given a plan and a CPS caseworker was assigned who followed all of us for the next year. But our daughter did not abide by the plan. One day the baby was asleep in her crib in another bedroom when I walked in on my daughter trying to shoot up heroin in our home. I immediately called CPS. The judge added a charge of neglect to my daughter's plan and required her to undergo long-term treatment, which she didn't complete.

When the baby was four months old, temporary custody was affirmed and at eighteen months, we were awarded full permanent custody. When our granddaughter was three-and-a-half years old, both biological parents agreed to have their parental rights terminated and we adopted our dear granddaughter. Now, at four and one-half, she is a happy, healthy well-adjusted child who attends pre-school and participates in ballet and soccer. We have continued to encourage contact with both biological parents. I am forever grateful they were able to put their daughter's best interests above their own.

Because of her exposure to heroin and methadone, we don't know if there will be learning issues or behavioral issues concerning our little girl. For now, she is just perfect and we are doing all we can to make her life as wonderful as possible.

My daughter has made numerous attempts at treatment but sadly, her struggle continues. She even suffered a serious overdose and survived. I don't want her to die but she can't seem to stay clean. I realize I am now a reluctant member of a club that I never dreamed I would join. I now live torn between a bittersweet ongoing fear for my daughter's life and the daily joy our granddaughter brings.

CHEMICAL WARFARE

Jennifer's Story

U nlike her three siblings, my youngest daughter was very rebellious growing up. She was eighteen when I learned she
was abusing drugs. Like any mother, I wanted so badly to get her
help and immediately began to look for answers. I contacted the
police for direction but they said since she was an adult, there was
nothing they could do. I called several rehabs but they wanted hun-
dreds of dollars up front and did not take insurance at the time.
The rehabs also required she admit she needed help before they
would take her, which was something she refused to do.

The discovery she was using crack cocaine terrified me. I hardly saw my daughter unless she needed something. She would sometimes return home without warning and then she wouldn't stay
long. One day she came into the house and lay down on the bed.
When I tried to wake her, she didn't respond. Fearing the worst, I
called 911. After examining her, the paramedics told me she was
coming down from crack and to let her sleep. Sure enough, she
woke up later and went on her way as if nothing had happened.
She couldn't understand what I had been worried about. It became
a challenge for me not to spend every minute of every day fearing
my daughter was soon going to die.

This continued for several years. But then things appeared to improve every time I saw her. She seemed to be looking better—or at least I thought she was. In fact, we even had some meaningful conversations together. So when she said she wasn't doing crack anymore—just smoking a little weed here and there—I believed her. Plus, she had a job.

During one of our conversations, she told me she stopped going to her friend's house because they were all doing heroin. Heroin? I hadn't heard that word since I was a teen and only when someone was talking about the "junkies" downtown. I knew nothing about this drug and was grateful she seemed to have enough sense to stay away from those people. My fears lessened somewhat and I started to feel a little better.

As time went on, her visits lessened, which I attributed to her being busy with her job so I completely understood. But I truly missed my baby girl. So in order to stay in touch with her, I bought her a cell phone. Even though we didn't see each other as often as I would have liked, she called me every night to say good night and I love you. But one night she didn't call. I panicked, thinking something must have happened, so I called her. She nonchalantly said she was sorry but she just forgot. This happened again the next night, and as much as I tried not to worry, I did.

A conversation with my younger son confirmed my heightening concerns when he said, "You know she's doing heroin, right?" I just looked at him in disbelief, as I stammered, "What? How do you know? She wouldn't do that. She told me she wouldn't. She was looking good and talking so nicely. No, it can't be!"

He let me get out all my words of denial out and then said, "Well, she doesn't look so good now." He told me when she was coming around to visit, she had just started using heroin and said in the beginning, heroin makes a person act very pleasant and seem normal.

As their drug use becomes heavier and they become more addicted, they begin to stay away. I guessed that was why I hadn't seen much of her, lately. I was devastated. He said he told her he knew what she was doing and wanted nothing to do with her until she stopped. He meant it. For the next five years, he didn't speak to his sister.

I will never forget the day he prophetically said to me, "Mom, she's going to get pregnant and you'll end up raising her baby." My immediate reaction to his statement was to dispel it. I honestly didn't believe that would ever happen. She loved kids, had always talked about being a mom and deep down I just knew she wouldn't chance getting pregnant while doing drugs—no way. Or so I thought.

The day I received her call saying, "Mom, I'm pregnant," my heart dropped. When I asked if she had stopped doing heroin, she said she was going to a doctor and he had put her on methadone. I figured if she was seeing a doctor all was well. But then she told me the doctor wanted to do a test because he thought the baby might have Down's syndrome. In my typical fashion, I reassured her. I told her not to worry. If the baby had problems, it would be fine and of course, I would help her.

A few months passed with no word from my daughter. But I heard through the grapevine she was still using. This information frustrated and angered me. This was not what I wanted to hear. Why do people feel they need to tell me these things? I couldn't do anything about it. I was sure they thought they were helping but my worry about my daughter and her unborn child made me crazy. I found myself becoming more stressed by this new information. I couldn't concentrate at work and began to have nightmares.

At last I received a call, but it was not from my daughter. Someone else called to let me know she was at the hospital having the baby. By the time I got there, the baby had already been born. There in the bassinette was a beautiful baby girl. She was so perfect. I gently put my hand on her chest and she reached out and grabbed my finger. My heart melted. I fell in love in that moment and promised her I would do everything in my power to keep her safe.

But dealing with my daughter was another story. Her boyfriend was with her. He was in withdrawal and sweating like crazy. My daughter was smiling and happy because they gave her pain pills. I asked her why they would do that? Didn't she tell them she was an addict? She just laughed at me.

"You were high when you came in here, weren't you?" I said. She laughed, again. "You'd better tell them now or I will," I said. But the doctors already suspected. My daughter tested positive for heroin. My sweet innocent granddaughter also tested positive for heroin, as well as cocaine and methadone. I flipped. She had used anything and everything she could while carrying the baby. I was beside myself.

Early the next morning, Children's Protective Services (CPS) called me and wanted to know if I'd be willing to keep my granddaughter. Of course, I said I would. I made her a promise to keep her safe and I was determined to keep it.

Almost immediately after birth, my granddaughter began having symptoms of withdrawal and was scheduled to stay at the hospital for three weeks in the Neonatal Intensive Care Unit for methadone therapy. My heart went out to her. This precious baby had endured drug abuse for nine months before she was even born and was now being given more drugs.

CPS charged my daughter with child endangerment and put her on a case plan. They asked me if I'd be willing to allow her to live in my home while she completed the plan of enrolling in the methadone clinic, going everyday and taking care of the baby, while I supervised her. If she did a good job, she wouldn't lose the baby. I consented to this as long as no drugs were being used. She agreed. But it didn't last long.

Every day, I was responsible for giving her twelve dollars for the cost of the methadone. She left each morning and was gone for five hours. I didn't know how those clinics worked and so I didn't even think to question her. I thought it was normal to be gone that long. One afternoon when she called me, I heard her screaming at someone in the background about "hits" and warned her that if she was back on drugs, not to come home. She didn't. Later, I found out she was giving the methadone money to her boyfriend and they were using it to get heroin. I called her caseworker and was told if she didn't come home in three days, she'd be charged with child abandonment, which would make the whole custody process easier for me. She didn't and I easily got custody.

Two months later, my daughter was busted in a drug raid and was charged with drug abuse and three counts of drug trafficking. Within twenty-four hours, however, she was released pending trial and I never even saw her. For her sentencing, she showed up high and the judge decided to keep her in jail. She went to prison for eighteen months.

I had no choice but to focus on throwing myself into taking care of my granddaughter, while still working to try to make a life for us. I wished with all my heart things were different and we could all be a family like it was supposed to be.

Meanwhile, I wrote my daughter every day in prison, sent pictures of her daughter, money, envelopes, etc. and made sure she had mail each day. Her letters to me were so encouraging. She was getting her high school equivalency diploma and had plans after her release to go to rehab, college, get a job and spend time with her daughter. It sounded so good. I was happy and relieved. However, the week before she was to be released, my anxiety returned. What if it didn't stick?

When she got out of jail and came home, she looked and sounded again like my daughter. I was elated. She immediately got busy contacting old friends who didn't do drugs, applied for a loan for school, was calling rehabs and putting in job applications at a very fast pace. I told her to slow down so she wouldn't get overwhelmed. Just three days later, she relapsed. She went back to her boyfriend and back to drugs. Eventually, she went back to the methadone clinic and has been there for the last four years. It's not ideal but it's keeping her alive. She sees her daughter occasionally and I only allow this because my granddaughter asks to see her. But the visits don't last long. My granddaughter always wants to come home after only a couple of hours.

In the midst of a multitude of challenges, my granddaughter and I have managed, but it hasn't been easy. Because my job required a lot of overtime and I couldn't find a sitter to accommodate all the extra hours, I was laid off. This actually turned out to be for the best. I needed the extra time for my granddaughter because she suffered serious repercussions of being a drug baby. She was diagnosed with Attention Deficit Hyperactivity Disorder, Oppositional Defiant Disorder, Sensory Processing Disorder and Mild Intellectual Disability.

Along with her many therapy appointments, I also had to enroll her in a virtual online school due to her behavioral problems. At almost nine years old, her intellectual development is that of only a six or seven-year-old. She is working very hard to catch up to her grade level and has a great attitude. In spite of everything, she is making great progress and doing very well. I love her so much. She is my heart and soul and I wouldn't trade a second of time with her for anything. I have raised four children and have thirteen grandchildren. But she has brought this fifty-nine-year-old more joy, love and laughter than I could ever have imagined. I need her in my life just as much as she needs me.

I will keep the promise I made to her in the nursery the day she was born. She is safe and most especially, she is loved. My granddaughter never asked to be a drug baby. I never asked to be a parent again. Sometimes it's the things we don't ask for that are the greatest gifts of all.

STRONG SOULS

Our grandchildren come to us with many complications and issues. But they also come to us with something stunningly beautiful—their souls. Over and over, we hear grandparents say how profound and sensitive their grandchildren are, perhaps because of what they've been through. They have an enlightenment about them that is deeper than other children and sometimes very unexpected, yet so delightful. Somehow these children seem to be the ones who nurture us more often than we ever dreamed, as well as teach and treasure us, as much as we do them. Great adversity can foster great rewards.

Julie's Story

My constant rock through the nightmare and turmoil in my life has been my incredible grandson, Kyler. From the very beginning, when I was supposedly the one who was supporting and teaching him—he began teaching me. He has taught me about resilience and overcoming circumstances we can't control. He has taught me about the freedom and power of forgiveness. He has taught me about the magnitude of faith. And most of all, he has taught me about selflessness. Because of him, I have been encouraged to be the best parent I can be. Yes, I said parent—not grandparent. It wasn't a title I wanted to take on but rather one he wanted to give me. Every kid out there wants a mom. I felt like if I allowed him to call me that, I was somehow dishonoring my daughter Emily's memory. But when I remarried, as part of our marriage vows, my pastor included the statement that Kyler had a "heavenly" mother, but I was his "earthly" mother. He also added he could now call my husband and me, Mom and Dad, which he has done since that day.

I guess because of Kyler's losses early in his life, he was more introspective than other children around his age. I have always encouraged dialogue about his mother and we've had many in depth conversations about his memories of her—good and bad. He's already lived through the worst so there really was no need in trying to shield him. I didn't just dump everything on him all at once, but I always answered his questions as honestly and age appropriately as I possibly could. I never gave excuses but rather offered probabilities and asked him what he thought. He was very insightful and sadly, he understood much more about addiction than any child ever should.

I would never have wished my life to turn out the way it has, but Kyler was a gift I couldn't have possibly have known otherwise. He has been the light at the end of the tunnel and the indisputable proof that all things really do work together for good.

IV

NEW SET OF ORDERS

"It is through the way you serve others
that your greatness will be felt."

—*Hawaiian Proverb*

SECOND TOUR OF DUTY

We realize we have been given a second chance and are committed to making the most of it. Many of us agree we're not doing things the same way we may have done them before. It's not easy to change our ways but with increased awareness and thought; it's happening. The grandchildren we're raising are better because of it and so are we.

Julie's Story

I keep asking myself to remember some of the crazy things I believed at fourteen. With that, I'm learning to bite my tongue and allow my now fourteen-year-old grandson/son to learn the important lessons in life for himself. After kids turn twelve, they don't think we know anything anyhow.

Sometimes I like to think Kyler is my "do over" child. He's given me the chance to impart things upon him I neglected to do the first time around. *Hello, and welcome to life lessons aka the things that have taken me fifty years to learn.*

As I watch him turn into the fine young man he is becoming, I know I deserve at least part of the credit. Some of this is due to my rearing and maybe even my "do over" mentality. But the rest is due largely to the fact he knew that when I said "forever," I meant it. Every child wants a forever home.

Security, stability and love can go a long way in changing the direction and ultimately, the outcome of children's lives. I am convinced of it. They don't have to become a statistic. Being born into addiction doesn't have to affect their destiny. It is we, the grandparents, who have stepped up to the plate to make that impact on their futures.

Are we different than other families? Yes, we are. But we are also becoming far more commonplace, as more grandparents are raising their grandchildren today than ever before. Is this what we had planned? Nope.

I remember a situation where Kyler got really mad at me several years ago and yelled, "I wish my real mom wasn't dead!" When he said that, part of me was so hurt and part of me was just down right angry. How dare he say something like that to me?

So I carefully gained my composure before I answered, mainly because there was a part of me that wanted to lash out and hurt him like he'd just hurt me. But I had to remind myself who the adult was. "I wish your real mom was alive too. I miss her everyday—just like you do," I answered. "It would have been great if she could have gotten her life together and raised you herself. I would have loved to have been the grandma and been able to do all of the fun things with you, instead of being the one that has to discipline you and make you do chores. But that's just not how it turned out."

We didn't speak to each other for probably an hour or more. Then he came to me, hugged me and told me he loved me. Nothing more had to be said. We had said enough. I think we both understood each other's frustrations a little better that day and how our lives had changed in that moment in time when Kyler and I came together.

Yes, we are different in so many ways as a family. But in other ways we are not. Kyler is anchored by the same love and commitment of any solid family. He has the same opportunities as any other child and is in no way defined by his mother's past. His mother's choices brought us together and he still has a mother's hand to hold his as long as he needs it. Mine.

GOOD DECISION

"Honesty is the best policy" is an idiom that suits every facet of life but is critical when raising children whose parents are addicts. Being truthful is a key element to gaining confidence with our new young charges. It's so important not to dance around the truth about their parent's addiction—especially important is letting them know it's not their fault. Validating their feelings in a matter-of-fact way releases their shame and brings comfort.

Lynne's Story

Brady's play therapist advised us to keep nothing secret and to make his history part of his life. That way, there would be no surprises and he'd grow up healthy. We listened and so far, it has paid off. Today, he is a happy and well-adjusted child who takes his uniqueness in stride. In fact, in fourth grade, when his teacher asked him to use one word to describe himself, he said he was "unique."

Earlier in first grade, his teacher told us how Brady always shared his story candidly with classmates and was very proud of who he was. We had told him many times who *we* were, but being only six years old, he seemed to have gotten confused.

Unexpected Heroes

Brady had just arrived home from school. Apparently, his first-grade classmates had been having a discussion about moms and dads because, out of the blue, our young boy took me aback with his question.

"So," he said with his hands on his hips, "what are you, my stepmother or what?"

Clearly, his friends were throwing terms at him trying to figure out who I was.

"No, Brady, I'm not," I answered. "Stepmothers aren't related to the children and you have my blood running through your veins."

He looked confused.

"Brady, I'm your grandmother; and because I take care of you, I'm also your mom. You have two in one!"

"How about Dad?" he queried.

"The same thing," I replied.

I could see the wheels turning while he was putting it all together.

"So let me get this straight," he self-assuredly re-capped. "In *real* life, if Jaime were still my mom, you'd be my grandmother. But because she took drugs and couldn't do it, you're my mom?"

"Yes," I replied.

Brady stood there very pensive. Then a smile of recognition slowly came on his face, as he nodded.

"God made a good decision."

MISFIT UNIFORM

Parenting for a second time is new territory. Suddenly, we are faced with the same physical challenges we encountered when we were young and raised our families along with our peers. The problem is we are no longer young. It's a foreign and very different place we've landed and as much as we try to fit in, the fit is sometimes questionable making for a mixed bag of emotions.

Mari's Story

I am sad and I am scared. I am lonely. I can't seem to find my place in the world.

Today, I was seated at an event with people my own age. I had nothing to say. I struggled to relate to them and they couldn't seem to relate to me. I, after all, was raising a child and wanted to talk about school starting, where to get the best price on a rolling backpack, how quickly the summer was going by, the vacation we took surrounding our child and ideas for a future vacation. They just wanted to talk about retirement and what they were doing to plan for it. We were on different planets.

Then I saw someone with a young child, and tried talking to her, but she didn't really care about talking to me. To her, I was probably someone who reminded her of her mother. I'm sure she thought, what could we have in common?

I've lost old friends, and potential friends somehow just stay potential friends. My older friends have lost patience because so many times we have had to find a sitter to go out with them and too often were forced to cancel plans because we couldn't. When we do get together, ensuing conversations are dominated by the comings and goings of raising a small child. They lose interest and rarely call anymore.

My potential friends are the parents of my grandson's friends. Sure, we talk about our kids and about school and about the project we're working on as volunteers. But we don't meet for lunch or go out for drinks or even girl talk on the phone. Consequently, I'm lost and I'm lonely. I feel like I'm trying to wear a uniform that doesn't fit.

Will this ever change? I love raising a child, again. I adore him and wouldn't trade my position for anything. But I worry I've lost myself along the way.

I am no longer the woman I once was. The woman who was aging nicely alongside her friends, laughing about past days together, sharing dinners and doing things they were doing. I looked forward to traveling and doing—whatever. But that's all changed; it had to. My interests and motivations have changed. All my thoughts are focused on raising this child and watching him grow into a happy fulfilled adult. The way it should be. The way it would have been for his mother, if she were still here.

Perhaps I must face I had my time in the sun and must now put my life on hold, while he grows up. I really don't even mind very much. But then what? I'm not sure I'll know how to move on. But I must figure it out soon because if I'm lonely and sad, it will affect him —and that's the last thing I want.

Maybe it's time to create a more satisfying life for myself now. Maybe I shouldn't wait for these younger friends to call me. Maybe it's time for me to take the reigns and invite them. If I don't make it happen, nothing will change and the uniform will never fit. I know I can do it. I must do it.

SHACKLED

We do what we have to do. It's the way most of us in our generation were programmed. We were told to suck it up, not complain and do the right thing. Trudge into unchartered territory and be victorious. Be a better person and the world will be a better place; even if what we each have to do changes life forever, as we know it.

Candace's Story

Because of poor choices my daughter made that caused her addiction and destroyed her ability to be a parent, I am currently raising my grandchildren. They came into my life over four and one-half years ago. My world immediately changed that day. I was back to changing diapers and getting up in the middle of the night. I had not done that in twenty years. I lost my freedom and was suddenly bound by school schedules, appointments and packing lunches. There would be no more "clean" house and that "alone" time I had gotten so used to, would be gone, along with dinner plans on a whim and adult vacations. What had I gotten myself into?

I often felt like I was living in a shaken snow globe. Addiction had upset my world, replacing clarity and order with murkiness and chaos. Since starting over again as a parent at age fifty-eight, I have often asked, "How can I go on?" Well, you do go on. And every day is a new challenge.

As if the adjustment to this new life wasn't hard enough, my older grandchild had learning disabilities, which took a lot of patience and a lot of appointments. My younger grandson had learning as well as behavioral disorders. He had misbehaved so many times at school, I dreaded seeing the school's number pop up on my phone. Some days I was so tired I couldn't even make it to bed at night and I would fall asleep on the couch.

My life was not what it was. No more freedom of just being able to get up and go somewhere. Florida trips with people my own age were a thing of the past. Friends no longer called and asked me to go out because they knew I had to find a baby sitter first. As far as retirement, I won't have that luxury until the youngest is eighteen. I'll be seventy-one.

But even with all the changes, all my losses, all the work and all the chaos, I have come to a realization. I would not change my life now for anything in this world. Above it all, I know I am doing something good. I am truly making a difference. I have direction and purpose. I am raising my grandchildren. What I have given up can't even compare.

CHANGE OF COURSE

Betty's Story

Since our grandson arrived, my life has been like a teeter-totter filled with ups and downs. He has brought us many challenges but also many joys. My husband and I had been the only constant in his life so when he officially came to us, it was not a hard transition for him. In fact, when he first found out he was going to be with us permanently, he was so happy to finally have his own sock drawer. He lined up all his little socks in a perfect little row. He had never had any organization or structure in his daily life and he was absolutely starving for it. He also arrived at our home so stressed out; he was constantly having accidents in his pants. But after just a few days, they stopped.

I know he still loves his mom and misses her, but he is thriving with us and I believe he is thankful we are here for him. Even now, with our lives turned upside down, knowing he appreciates us; makes it easier for my husband and I to do our jobs.

We did have a different future plan, though, and had to completely change our course. We had worked hard and saved money for our retirement years. Suddenly that was all out the window. We were raising a child, again—the last thing I wanted to be doing. We could no longer pick up and go anywhere or do whatever we wanted whenever we wanted because our lives were structured around caring for our eight-year-old grandson. I know it might sound selfish, but I was looking forward to the day when I could finally focus on myself. I lost myself along the way and needed time to be my own caretaker and find myself again. Instead, I was back to packing lunches, homework, teacher conferences, doctor visits, play dates and sleepovers. And planning birthday parties— sometimes I felt like I would rather go to the dentist.

My husband, on the other hand, was delighted to have a boy in the house. He never had the chance to raise a son and now had that chance. He bought a race kart and involved our grandson in racing. Becoming a good driver has done wonders for his self-esteem. It's an activity that brings our new little family together. My husband is having a ball and living vicariously through our grandson and feels he has a purpose.

I really must admit, this past year was the best I've had in a long, long time. My daughter was in prison, the bio dad was in prison, the boyfriend was in prison and I could finally sleep at night. I didn't have one nightmare, and I actually started to have fun and enjoy life again. This was the first year I felt comfortable taking a vacation and not fearing some druggie would break into my home while I was gone.

Feeling a bit of freedom, we decided to take our grandson to the beach for a week and it was the best rejuvenating holiday— truly what we needed. My grandson insisted on bringing some of the beach home in a plastic bag. He touches it once in a while and says, "I love you. I had the best time!" It just warms my heart we could bring some joy and normalcy into his life. And it was beyond wonderful to begin to find myself, again.

As much as I wish his parents could understand this, they just don't get it. It angers me they put drugs before their precious child and I have to sometimes pretend everything is fine for our grand-child, while I'm really just feeling sad his parents aren't around. But through this gamut of emotions, as long as I focus on our grand-son, it helps to level things out because I know we are doing the right thing. In my mind and in my heart, I know it's better they're not here.

My daughter's safe in prison, but I dread the day she gets out. We talk on the phone once a week. She is clear-headed and the con-versations are pleasant. But once she is freed, this will all change. I will have to be strong again with the boundaries I have set with her. I hate the thought of my daughter living in a homeless shelter, but she has to find her own way without any help from us. Even though she has begged to come live here with us, we have repeat-edly told her no. It would be impossible for me to have her under my roof again, so we are standing firm.

Enough is enough and I have had enough. She talks like she is beginning to understand and is seeking other options. I need to get out of her way and let her live her life however she chooses. I have discussed this with our grandson and he understands why his mommy can't be here. He is now ten years old and we have decided honesty is best and have explained everything to him in an age appropriate way. The last time it came up he said, "I understand Mommy can't live here, but do I *have* to go live with her?" I said, "No baby, of course not." His answer was, "Good. I like it here with you and Papa." Mixed emotions…and the teeter-totter goes up and down again.

DRAFTED

We never asked to parent our children's children but agreed to accept the job without reservation. No one would ever choose to walk in our shoes, but after dealing so long with the challenges of having addict children, no one could be better equipped to raise our grandchildren. Our love for them is carefully honed by a unique understanding of their innocence and value, in addition to a desire to do everything possible to prevent them from walking the same path as their parents.

Karen's Story

I received custody of my two-month-old granddaughter in January. Child Protective Services (CPS) had been involved since the day she was born.

Although my daughter had a history of drug use, I didn't know she had tested positive the previous September for meth, while she was pregnant. When she was admitted to the hospital to give birth, she tested negative so I assumed she had been able to stay clean and sober. She seemed so happy, so normal. She certainly fooled me.

After the baby's birth, CPS gave her every opportunity to take parenting classes and test clean before they took the baby. She failed miserably.

My daughter had been living with me prior to her pregnancy and during that time I had no idea she was using again. I worked the night shift full time so I was usually at work or would often be sleeping during the day. I honestly didn't know because as far as I could see, my daughter was doing a good job taking care of her baby.

However, this quickly changed the day I woke up to my daughter holding the phone saying CPS wanted to talk to me. As soon as I said hello, they informed me that because of her non-compliance, they had to take the baby. My daughter begged them to leave her with me and told them she would be the one to leave our home. They asked me if I would be willing to take the baby. Of course, I said yes.

But before giving me the infant, I had to go through a detailed background check that made me feel like a criminal myself. My heart broke as I watched my daughter walk out the door with only the clothes on her back, and then again when CPS took the baby so that they could check me out. I never felt so shattered and alone in my life. Thankfully, it was just five hours before they brought my granddaughter back home to me. But my daughter was now homeless and there was nothing I could do about that. I couldn't fix the situation and I couldn't fix her.

My insurance paid for only thirty days of rehab and my daughter procrastinated going for almost a month. Once she was there, I tried to convince her to ask the county to pay for more time. I knew she wasn't ready to leave, but she refused to stay longer. When she left rehab, she stayed sober for a little over a month. She had moved in with her dad and was going to her aftercare and meetings, but just couldn't stay away from the "bad people."

Her dad let her use one of his vehicles to get back and forth to classes and during that time it was stolen twice. The first time was by a "friend." I found the car and returned it to her father. The second time I didn't even bother looking. I had thought living with him was a bad idea and strongly felt she should have gone to a sober living facility. I hated being right about that. It didn't take long for her to leave her father's house. She didn't return.

During the following four weeks, she was kicked out of the class she was required to take for a drug misdemeanor she received months before she was pregnant. Then she tried a new program through Social Services to help her stay clean. This program involved taking classes three times a week, a scheduled drug test once a week, random drug testing during the week, as well as court every Friday to see a judge. Even so, I didn't see her being able to do this while still living in a bad environment with easy access to the wrong people.

When CPS did their monthly check on the baby, I told them my daughter had been kicked out of her court-ordered class for her misdemeanor charge. I also told them I didn't think she was ready to be a mom. They agreed. They had previously asked me if I would be willing to adopt if it came down to that. Of course I told them I would. When they asked this same question again, my answer remained "Yes." I cried because I never wanted my daughter to lose her little girl. I so wanted her to experience the joy of being a mom. There was no dad in the picture to make things complicated. Both men who could have been the daddy, hid from Social Services so they wouldn't have to take a paternity test. They didn't want child support payments.

Now, drafted into a war I never chose to fight, every day continues to be a struggle for me because I am once again, a single mom when I didn't choose to be one. I worry for my own little girl out on the streets, but I know there is nothing I can do for her.

She has to want help and ask for it. She has to do it herself. I can't enable her. Her little girl is my top priority now. I was a single mom of two children before and I can do it again. I come from a long line of strong women. I know I can find the strength.

YELLOW RIBBON

Unexpected heroes come in many forms. While it's common to see the matriarch of the family stepping directly into the line of fire similar to a mother bear protecting her cubs, our patriarchs must also be recognized. Without the advantage of being pre-programmed with maternal instincts, they often must make the greatest change in the course of their lives when the responsibility of raising another child becomes theirs.

Lar Lei's Story

My sixty-year-old husband seemed willing and ready to take on parenting our granddaughter when the unexpected and unthinkable happened to our family. But I was still apprehensive. After all, he had never had a child and this was far from being planned.

Even though my ex-husband and his wife agreed to take care of my addict son's son, I was sorry they couldn't take both children forcing us to split the siblings up. But at least we could be there for his little girl.

On the way back from Tennessee with my granddaughter, I was worried and truly hoped my husband would be able to do this.

Unexpected Heroes

But once we arrived back in Florida, I was filled with relief. My husband looked down at my granddaughter smiling and she looked up at him. Then she immediately grabbed a hold of his hand and instantly bonded to him.

Unfortunately, I caught a cold in Tennessee, a bad one. I was so sick. It was all I could do to breathe. My husband, who was working from home, jumped right in and handled everything. Remember, he'd never had kids in his sixty years of life, but it was as if he'd had a dozen. This wonderful man was so gentle and understanding of this scared little girl whom he loved at first sight. He understood when bedtime frightened her because she couldn't see when she took off her glasses. The pictures on the wall looked like blood dripping to her, so Papa took them down.

With my husband in the lead, we researched private and public schools and enrolled her in a Montessori. We updated her shots, filed for power of attorney and took care of every other detail that popped up. Then, that first weekend she was with us, she got strep throat. My husband nursed her and comforted her as if she was his own child. The end of the following week we took her to the eye doctor for a check-up. They discovered she had an elongated optic nerve and sent us straight to the hospital for a lumbar puncture and CAT scan to rule out a potentially serious problem (which, fortunately, all turned out normal).

Now called "Papa," my husband stayed by our granddaughter's side in the hospital the entire night as well as the next day while I went to work. She was released from the hospital Halloween night and it was Papa who held her while she sobbed because she didn't get home in time to wear her Elsa dress and go Trick or Treating. A few nights later she woke up in the middle of the night with a headache and severe pain in her back and leg, screaming, "Make it stop, make it stop!" We drove her to the ER and the entire time,

161

my husband held her wrapped in a blanket. Ibuprofen stopped the pain and it was diagnosed as something that sometimes happens as a side effect after a lumbar puncture.

That weekend, her headaches continued. Sunday we took a picnic lunch to the park, but she threw up from the pain. The next day she still was not better so we took her back to the hospital. They sent her home to lay flat on her back for the headaches. If that didn't work, they informed us they would have to do a dangerous procedure called a blood patch. But, gratefully, it worked.

Through all of these initial emergencies she held on to my hand and especially to Papa's hand. He was her prince. She responded to us and to our friends who welcomed her. She blossomed. She was loved. Her needs were finally being met. She trusted us. Soon, she was sleeping on her own with absolutely no fears. We brought stability to her life and she brought meaning to ours. My husband, who was clearly always meant to be an amazing father, remains her shining prince and she will always be his princess. For that, I am more grateful than I can ever say.

BRAVEHEART

Lynne's Story

A t first, Stu thought it was gas, an ulcer or perhaps even his
heart. He'd already suffered one heart attack and had more
than his share of angioplasties. Still, we were fairly convinced his
heart was okay. After several check-ups and tests with negative results, he concluded it must be a strained back and went for physical
therapy. But our relief was short-lived when the physical therapist
felt a mass that was eventually diagnosed (after too many months
of testing) as non-Hodgkin's abdominal lymphoma. The news was
devastating. But it was especially upsetting to my engineer husband
who now was saddled with something else he couldn't control.
After everything he'd already been through with our addict daughter, it was hard to accept another hurdle, particularly with her son
as our newest full-time responsibility. How were we going to do
this? Our grandson was just three years old. My husband was getting ready to go through chemo and Brady was in the middle of
the terrible threes. How were we going to find the quiet and focus
necessary to support a healing atmosphere in our home in the face
of so much stress?

Stu was scared and didn't know if he could handle it all. He
tried to hint to me perhaps another arrangement for Brady should

be made. But I didn't want to listen. I had my walls up, not able to face his disease on top of everything else I had not handled particularly well. I would drive him to chemo but couldn't be around it, so I left and ran errands—anything for distraction. Stu thought it was insensitive and uncaring. I saw it as survival. Overwhelmed by Stu's illness, I needed my wits about me to care for Brady in as positive a light as possible. I wish I could have done both.

I had just brought Stu home after his second round of chemo when he weakly said, "Lynne, I don't think I can go through this and raise Brady at the same time." Stu said going through chemo was like having a major flu that never went away. He felt so sick, so lethargic and in such pain he thought we should have Brady go to one of our other adult children's homes. But I couldn't agree. "Please Stu, we can't do that to him," I begged. "He's been through enough upheaval in his short little life. We have to make this work."

Stu nodded and said okay. But I knew he was just too weak to argue and would probably ask again. The next day, we had planned a hair-shaving party so when he began losing his hair, Brady wouldn't be afraid. Our youngest son, Josh, came over to do the job. Stu sat on our staircase, while Josh made jokes as Stu's hair fell to the floor. Brady thought it was hilarious seeing Stu's head shaved and his laughter lit up the room. Afterwards, Brady lovingly climbed up on Stu's lap, threw his arms around his neck and patted his sad baldhead. "Please, don't worry. I love you. You'll be fine," our insightful little man said in the sweetest three-year-old voice.

Stu's eyes welled up with tears. "I think Brady's the one who's going to get me through this," he surrendered.

At that moment I saw my husband clearly for what was maybe the first time in our lives. After years of unthinkable horror in the midst of dealing with two addicted children, he truly was the quiet strength that kept us going. Even sick and extremely weak he knew he couldn't abandon Brady or ignore my desire to keep him. I had always thought of myself as the warrior in our family as Stu often sat back and let me do the fighting. But I suddenly realized I was only able to fight so hard because of him. Life happens and sometimes addiction and cancer, sadly even together, are part of that.

Stu completed his treatment and Brady greeted him with loving arms after every session, along with sweet reassurances he would be okay. Even so young, he seemed to understand his supportive role in Stu's recovery. Today, my dear brave husband is eight years cancer-free and gratefully, his heart disease has been quiet. He has been an amazing dad to Brady, doing the job even better the second time around. His devotion to Brady and to me is something we cherish and we both feel so blessed he is here to share life with us.

BACK IN THE TRENCHES

Maturity and experience have many benefits. We take things in stride better than in our younger days and can draw on the lessons of the past to help us face the future. We know the value of patience and sacrifice. Are we perfect? No, certainly not. But one thing is for sure, we have become very good at making lemons into lemonade...

Kani's Story

I've been married to the love of my life, my high school sweetheart and most amazing man on earth, for five years. Reading this, you'd probably think I'm twenty-something, right? Nope. I'm fifty-one.

Sixteen years ago, we both wound up divorced at the same time. We became friends and eventually fell in love. But he had custody of his three kids and I had my two. We lived in different towns thirty miles apart. We knew it would be difficult to combine households because we had very different parenting styles. But more important, we knew our kids had been through enough and we wanted to put them first. So we talked on the phone every night and saw each other on the weekends. Supporting each other through single parenting, we knew it would be at least twelve years before we could get married. But we also knew when that time came it would be worth it. We could put each other first and simply be newlyweds, grandparents, travelers, and just enjoy life.

So we waited. We eventually had our last child grown and we finally got married. The first two years we were able to do all those things we planned to do. We could cook a big dinner or just eat cereal if we wanted. We could jump out of bed Saturday morning, hop in the car and go to Dallas for the day. We could go to the movies at the drop of a hat. We could sleep until noon. We could pick the grandkids up and spoil them rotten and then take them back home. Life was grand and we deserved it. After all, we had done the right thing by our kids and put ourselves on the back burner for twelve long years.

Then my daughter, who had a history with drugs but had been clean for four years, did not just fall off the wagon—she dove off—straight into a "not breathing and unresponsive" ride in an ambulance to the ER. Child Protective Services (CPS) immediately became involved and her son came to stay with us until she could get her life back in order. A tumultuous eight months followed which included her fourth trip to rehab, and then she was back. She had a nice apartment, not so nice car, a job and we were slowly integrating our grandson back into her life. Then she nose-dived again. Another couple of weeks of the usual suspicions on my part and once again, she was back in the ER. It was her second overdose in a year. CPS tried to start the process again with her but this time she refused to cooperate.

After a few months, we were told if we did not take action to get custody of our grandson, the State would intervene. We went to court and were granted custody. Meanwhile, she and her boyfriend went to the Metroplex and lived out of her car until it was impounded, were arrested for copper theft and were in and out of jail for probation violations.

So now my husband and I found ourselves cooking a meal every night, going to basketball and baseball practice, missing work if the schools were closed, getting up early on Saturday morning and having to find and pay for a babysitter if we wanted to go out to dinner or a movie. This time, I didn't get to spoil my grandson and send him home. I got to ground him if he got an "orange" at school, did homework every night with him and made him clean his room. And for the first six months, I got to hear him cry, "I want my mommy!" whenever I punished him for anything. Then I got to explain his mommy loved him but she didn't make good decisions so it was safer for him to live with us. I also got to feel terribly guilty because my wonderful husband did not sign up for this.

There were days when I was incredibly resentful of all we had suddenly lost…and there were days when I was so angry with my daughter I couldn't see straight…and days when I tried to figure out what it was I must have done wrong with her…and finally, days when I had to feel the sting of disapproval from my own parents for my detachment from her drama and her disorder. To them she was still their precious granddaughter whom I had abandoned. But to me, she was an addict who brought unsafe, criminal threats to our life. We simply couldn't be involved with her because above all else we had to provide a safe and secure environment for my grandson.

But on these days when I was feeling particularly sorry for myself, I would read a story about a child who had died at the hands of a man the mother allowed into her child's life or I would read about a sixty-year-old grandmother who was single and raising four of her grandkids alone and I knew it could absolutely be worse. On those days, I thanked God we were able to take care of this precious life with whom we had been entrusted. I felt Him telling me that I didn't do anything wrong at all but that He had chosen me. And I knew that everything was part of a plan I couldn't see or understand because His ways are not our ways and in spite of everything this brought me great comfort.

V

OPERATION
GRAND FAMILY

⁓

"If I could tell you one thing,
It would be
You're never as broken as you think you are.
You have scars and sad memories.
But then again...
All great heroes do..."

—*AUTHOR UNKNOWN*

BASIC TRAINING

When we first became parents, there was no training manual we could consult. Like generations before us, we had to wing it. Drawing from our own upbringing, most of us naturally continued those strategies and behaviors with our own children. Some were good and some were not. Taking the time to examine the way we were raised before raising our own children was not always an option. Many of us were young and reared our children by the seat of our pants.

Even more so, raising grandchildren is a new frontier with no instructions and no map to guide us. Simply dropped in our laps, the job of parenting our grandchildren was more complex this time around for a variety of reasons. Unlike the autonomy we had with our first family, our grandchildren's bio parents, often make our job even more challenging.

To complicate things further, the generation of kids we're raising is different from our own children. To say times have changed is an understatement. Our grandkids are growing up in a fast-paced digital world and we have no choice but to keep up.

It would certainly benefit us to be younger and faster on our feet. On the other hand, our years of experience have taught us patience and an understanding of the big picture younger parents may not have. This, along with our love for them, gives us what we need to do our jobs. And this time around, we'll do it even better.

Lynne's Story

Raising our grandson as a three-parent family with our daughter living in the house was tricky, to say the least. When she relapsed and left for sober living, we thought it might become easier, but that wasn't the case. My husband and I had to face this new territory head on, while my daughter skillfully complicated the job we had to do. She was constantly calling us from the sober living home, ranting and criticizing us for how we were raising her son. "Don't forget to match his clothing," she'd admonish. "Put his blue-striped hat with his navy outfit." That's what was important to her and most likely, the only way she could feel she had any control while we had her son.

Our daughter was also fearful, especially because her baby was now a toddler and would soon develop into a growing child with more important needs. We'll always believe that's why she had to escape again into the world of drugs, before he was two. Although she left most of the responsibility to us, she understandably still wanted the title of mother.

The day she left for sober living, she said, "Don't forget, I'm his mother—*not you.*" With those words, she threw a flyer at me about local meetings for something called G.A.P. She didn't read it clearly and she thought the acronym stood for Grandparents *and* Parents, thinking it would help me see my place with her son. But it stood for Grandparents *as* Parents. And, in fact, I did go to the meetings. The weekly gatherings gave me information, peer support and clarity about how to go about my newly acquired role. The group was my lifesaver and gave me my basic training for everything I needed along the way.

Being called Mommy and Daddy by a three-year-old in public turned heads. I'm a little younger-looking than my chronological age, but not *that* younger-looking. I felt a bit self-conscious and wondered what people were thinking. I tried to "act" younger, smiling to hide the fine lines on my face and being spryer on my feet, even though my back was hurting. But I didn't fool anyone. Fitting in will always be a hurdle and something that will never be truly comfortable. The age difference is sometimes an issue with the younger parents and we no longer have much in common with our peers. It's a work in progress, but I'm learning to relax, accept my age and be myself.

As saddened as I was losing my daughter when Brady was five and one-half, I must admit her passing made our job less complicated and less stressful. Brady hadn't seen her in almost three years when she passed. He was naturally upset, but his memory of her had faded so it was less traumatic, though he will most likely always feel a void. Fortunately, we've been around him since birth, which made the transition easier and he loves we adopted him.

Of course, I miss my daughter's sweet essence before drugs and wish things had been different. But my husband and I have embraced our new roles with a positive attitude.

We have learned to parent differently from our first time around. Not being a traditional family, I believe we try harder and are more protective of our now son. We spend more time being with him instead of trying to go out somewhere without him. Because I am no longer working, I have had the luxury of being involved as homeroom parent and helping with school activities, something I couldn't do when I parented my first family. Since my husband retired, he's even assisted with baseball coaching, which he didn't have time for when he was in the throes of work. We're more relaxed as parents than we were with our other kids, welcoming Brady's friends to the house at any time or simply just being in his company. As his parents, we obviously have had to become his disciplinarians, but still hold onto the unconditional love and delight we feel as grandparents. Raising this child, our ego has been removed and we've been able to sit back and let him be who he is; nurturing his talents, rather than molding him into something we'd *like* him to be.

Still, because of our ages, it's not always easy putting all this effort into a child. There are days we're just tired and long for a leisure life. But his life has become more important to us. Even so, time remains our enemy, and we hope we will be here to see our young son blossom into a fine man. Perhaps, instead of inventing a manual for raising grandchildren, we should be working on a way to restore time.

BOOT CAMP

H-h-h-Homework? We have to help with homework, again. Again? Of all the things we have to face as grandparents raising grandchildren, homework has to be one of the most dreadful. It's the last thing we wanted at this stage of our lives, but it can't be avoided. Even the younger parents complain with a vengeance, especially because it's being given at an earlier age. Even kindergarten children are bringing work home.

And then there is math. Never a fan favorite, but today, children have to master a variety of ways to solve the same problem. Why? Why change something that isn't broken? And the ranges of methods seem to change with every season. We're older and change isn't easy. Even so, we trudge on and painfully attempt to learn the new concepts right along with our grandkids.

Technology is another challenge that is still as foreign to some grandparents as it is normal to our gadget-loving grandkids. We have no choice but to adapt. Many of us have not only learned to be computer savvy, but have learned to skillfully play video games and have even mastered texting.

It's a whole new world, but it's also just one more thing to do. And one more thing to do, among all the things we're now back to doing, is sometimes almost too much...

Teresa's Story

I wish it wasn't true, but most days I feel like a grouch instead of a loving, fun grandma. It's so stressful waking up at five o'clock every morning to be ready for the day. I lay my grandkids clothes out the night before, so there's minimal decision-making when I get them up at six because then it's non-stop with the children who are four, seven and twelve years of age. It's pure chaos and a constant battle for me during the school week.

"No, you can't wear shorts. It's thirty degrees outside," I say. "No, you did not brush your teeth. The brush is dry! And please put on deodorant," I beg. "You're growing up." After they're dressed and their hair is in place, it's time for a quick breakfast of frozen waffles, cereal or toast and jelly, as I'm scolding; "At the table—not in the living room!"

It's time to get to school. We look for jackets and the kids shove papers into their backpacks before I ask, "Did anyone let the dog out?" Of course, the answer is, as always, "It's not my turn." We're just about out the door when I hear the twelve-year-old scream, "Grandma, hurry up and come here—the dog made a mess on the floor!" Then he quickly switches topics and says, "Oh, and Grandma, I need to bring in canned goods for the homeless kids today." As I grab something from the pantry and hand it to him, he asks, "What is coconut milk? Can't I just bring something *normal?*"

While I try to ignore this last request, the seven-year-old yells from the other room, "Grandma, I need you to sign this permission slip that's due today for our field trip and I need six dollars." Just as I'm rummaging through my purse for dollar bills, I hear, "Oh, and I almost forgot—you need to sign this test so the teacher knows you know I got an F." While processing that news, the four-year-old sweetly says, "Look, Grandma, I made this for Mommy.

It's a rainbow. When will she be home? I miss Mommy." I let out a huge sigh and respond, "I know, honey. I do too."

So I clean up the dog's mess, put the dishes in the sink, pack lunches, handout money and sign notes before taking the four-year-old to daycare. The other two walk to school. Before they leave, I remind them, "Make sure you turn off all of the lights and the TV!"

"We will."

Yeah, right, I'm thinking. It's exactly why my electric bill has more than doubled.

When we arrive at the daycare, I sign my four-year-old in and she's smiling. She really likes it there. I give her one more kiss, a hug and she runs off with her friends while I head off for phase two of my day.

This is actually the easy part. I'm a manager at a Fortune 500 company and the pace is challenging and non-stop, but it's easy compared to the rest of my day. Here, I know the rules, the players and the game. I work hard and am recognized for my work. It is comfortable. That is, until the phone rings and displays the daycare's name. The four-year-old is sick and needs to be picked up immediately. If not that, it's often the grade school. The twelve-year-old said something inappropriate at recess or the seven-year-old forgot his permission slip. Didn't I just sign it?

By five o'clock, I'm yawning at work, preparing myself for phase three, the toughest part of my day. Before leaving, I check my calendar for the evening's schedule: child psychologist at six, soccer practice at seven and basketball practice at eight. On the drive home, I figure out how to fit dinner, homework and baths into the schedule while keeping my fingers crossed the ice cream truck doesn't drive by to throw the whole house into a frenzy.

It's the end of the day I feel like I have become such a grouch. And then I think I get to do it all again tomorrow. Good thing they know I love them. And I really do—even more than I ever imagined.

PERFECT STORM
OF HARDSHIP

"Are you kidding? It's *how much* to get her car out of impound?" the mother of an addict child asks.

Aside from the emotional overhaul addiction causes, it can also deplete and devastate a family financially. Fiscal demise can begin with the addict child but many times it can trickle down to the parent, who may be trying to rectify the financial mess their child has created.

Rehab programs, rent, sober houses, lingering parking or traffic tickets, court costs and impounded cars are just a few of the debts frequently incurred by parents of addicts who should be focusing on their own financial security as they face their retirement years. While it's easy to argue financially supporting an adult child is enabling—financial stress is no less easy to navigate than other forms of enabling.

Raising an addict's child or children could possibly be considered the greatest debt assumed by another person. This combined with the addict child's other incurred debt can create a perfect storm of hardship. There is minimal financial support available for grandparents raising grandchildren.

Even under normal circumstances, raising a child can be a financial challenge. But if the children have special needs and must have individual psychological, therapeutic or educational support, costs can become overwhelming. Nonetheless, time after time, grandparents will do whatever is necessary to give their grandchildren what they need even at the sacrifice of their own financial security.

Pattee's Story

When my daughter was healthy, she was extremely responsible, especially with her finances. She even helped her boyfriend improve his credit after he filed for bankruptcy. She made sure his bills were paid on time and, utilizing her great money management skills, got him out of debt. Her frugality helped her buy a car, provide well for her children and settle into a lovely rental home with a nice yard.

So when she gradually began failing to pay her bills and needed me to help get her through the month financially—I began to suspect something was terribly wrong. She had always been the one child in our family who didn't depend on us for money. She never failed to pay her own way. Because of her excellent history, we initially didn't begrudge her some help. In return, she was careful to pay us back, usually within just a few days.

But then the repayment days started to stretch out until they stopped all together. She had been a valued employee and her employer gave her many chances, until he had no choice but to terminate her. That's when we discovered our daughter was addicted to drugs.

Learning this and out of concern for my grandchildren's welfare, I tried to obtain guardianship. Because my daughter had no job and no income and because I had filed for guardianship, she would now also lose her home. In hopes someday she might be able to regain custody, I wanted her and the children to have a place to which to return. So in the interim, I helped pay for her rent and utilities to keep her place intact.

We were fortunate to have health benefits that covered free intervention, detox and an inpatient treatment program. An interventionist we asked to help us wanted my daughter to agree to go into a rehab. Unfortunately, his method for getting her there was to use any means he could. He enticed her by lying and saying he'd pay her bills while she was there, just so she would go. Even though drugs were still a priority with our daughter, some sense of her old responsibility remained. She was still concerned about leaving for three months without a way to get her affairs in order, so he had found the perfect ploy.

As soon as I realized he had no intention of helping her with this, but instead had deceptively planned for her to lose everything, which he considered to be a natural consequence for her actions; I jumped in and covered her expenses without her knowledge. It was my way of supporting her since I felt he had betrayed her. Although I was criticized for enabling, I'm not sure that was what it was for me. I couldn't see how his methods could possibly be productive. If she was able to get clean and then learned she had lost everything—believing it was being taken care of—she would have been devastated.

Thankfully, she did go into the rehab. But just before leaving for treatment, her car was impounded. It was accruing more fees every day, so while she was away, we planned to get it out of the impound facility. Numerous times a day, I went to the police station waiting for the faxed signature from her that was supposedly being sent allowing the release of the car to me. But day after day it didn't come. I soon found out it was because she had run away from the facility. In fact, she ran three times and ultimately did not return. I eventually got the car by paying much more than it was worth. Again, I had been burned financially and promised myself this would be the last time. But the damage was already done.

With my finances in dire straights, I had to work twelve-hour days and would not be able to retire for some time. I had to pay off the debts incurred by my altruistic effort to help my daughter, along with the legal fees for five months of court hearings for guardianship of her children. I had spent well over twelve thousand dollars in an effort to try to support my sick child, clean up her wreckage, save my grandbabies and prepare for their future. Her financial consequences were now firmly in the laps of my husband and myself. My once frugal, fiscally responsible girl had destroyed her credit, as well as mine. She had lost everything and I was fighting just to keep my head above water.

I could do nothing to save her. She completely left the responsible world in which she previously lived. Therefore, I had to turn away from my baby in order to save the rest of us.

I counted the months before I would be finished paying off the attorney so I could return to paying off previous debts. My sixty-five-year-old husband wanted to retire but there was no way he could. I was self-employed and would also have liked to retire soon, but our financial future looked bleak. Instead of building for our own retirement, we were paying for piano lessons, soccer lessons, zip line experiences, clothes, field trips, doctor visit deductibles, co-pays, dental visits, lunch snacks, gifts, toys, equipment, not to mention going through at least two loaves of bread a week and several gallons of milk.

We received no aid. And since our youngest is just six years old, we have many years ahead of us. While we initially thought this arrangement might be temporary, we now believe it's probably permanent. Our daughter seems to have abandoned her children completely, something previously thought by everyone who knew her to be unimaginable. Drugs changed her, like so many others, into a monster. They sucked the personality, character and the very soul right out of her. And unhappily, we ended up paying the price.

COMPASSION FATIGUE

Often, it's the matriarch of the family who feels the most respon-sible for the family's happiness, both individually and collectively. This is especially true when family dynamics change due to drug addiction. But the pressure of this responsibility combined with a loss of important boundaries can cause compassion fatigue.

Compassion fatigue, known as the "cost of caring," is caused by profound emotional and physical exhaustion that can be experienced when dealing with a drug-addicted family member and/or even tak-ing care of an unexpected child or children. Compassion fatigue is di-rectly linked to empathy and how we connect emotionally with others.

When the main caretaker of the family goes beyond the point of no return through their efforts to care for, ac-cept responsibility or even financially support another family member—seen often in homes with addicted children—that caretaker can frequently be prone to accidents, increased fa-tigue, loss of concentration, poor self-esteem, disturbed sleep patterns, nightmares, anger and outbursts, along with a sense of hopelessness. Compassion fatigue can look like depression and mimic the symptoms, so it is important to seek professional advice if these symptoms persist.

Central to compassion fatigue is a person's ability to tap into em-pathy. Empathy encompasses three important things: knowing what another is feeling, feeling what another is feeling, and responding compassionately to another person's distress. And much like codependency, this can unconsciously threaten wellbeing. The more empathetic someone is, the more likely it is that they will mirror their loved ones by taking on their emotions and his or her emotional state.

Imagine for a moment a confrontation you may have had recently with your loved one. Did you walk away frowning and tense? Did you somehow feel displaced and off-center due to the tension? Were you suddenly depressed or unexpectedly anxious? You were absorbing their emotions. When your face holds a certain emotion, such as a frown, your body is tricked into thinking it's mad. If you were to hold a pencil between your teeth to fake a smile then your body would think it was happy. The same principle is in effect when we mirror body language and especially the emotions of others.

One way to be protected from compassion fatigue is to consciously change your body language during difficult conversations. Another way is to be more diligent than ever in taking care of you by getting enough rest, healthy food, and exercise. Taking up a hobby and keeping positive social connections have also been shown to reduce the impact of compassion fatigue.

As mothers and family members of addicts as well as parents to their children, we are at great risk for suffering from compassion fatigue. Awareness of the warning signs is imperative to our emotional and ultimately our physical health.

Mari's Story

All I've ever wanted was for my family to be healthy, happy and loving—in life and with each other. As the mother of three children, it seemed to be my mission and I was bent on doing anything I could for my goal to be reached. Unfortunately, I didn't know I'd lose myself in the process.

I was always in sync with my kids. I made it my business to be on top of their business, thinking that's what a good mother did. But I took it to the extreme. I thought the more involved I was, the better I could help them navigate through life, seeing through their eyes while guiding them with my wisdom. But that didn't work. It just made me crazy. If one of my children came home hurt, I was hurt and if one was angry, I was angry. Instead of helping them understand the situation, I commiserated with them and found myself being defined by how my children were feeling. I'm sure I was just seen as one of those "super moms" who prioritized supporting everything their children did from homework to sports; even dating. I was convinced I was doing the right thing and so far it seemed to be working as one after another of my kids seemed to excel.

But then the tables were turned on me when we discovered one of my "perfect kids" was a drug addict. Because I was already so vested in her and felt her so deeply; her addiction felt like betrayal to me and I was overwrought. I didn't sleep well, suffered anxiety some days and depression others. I gained weight and completely stopped doing anything I enjoyed.

I felt horrible about myself and completely engulfed in self-blame for everyone's problems, not just those of my daughter. I looked to my other children for solace but they were angry with my daughter and even angrier with me for seeming to allow my daughter's behavior. In fact, my son actually accused me of being too weak to tell her "no" and I resented him for that. But deep down I knew he was right. He felt betrayed by the lack of support he received while all my energy went to his sister. I knew I couldn't continue what I was doing but just didn't have any idea how to stop. The worse she became, the harder I tried to fix her as well as try to keep my family in check at the same time. I knew I was headed for a breakdown. I knew I just couldn't do it anymore.

Out of desperation I broke down and went to a therapist; something I had always taken pride in not needing in my life. But somehow just the act of doing something just for me made a difference. Slowly I began to understand I couldn't control my daughter's actions and also had to let go of everything else I was trying to control. I also accepted loving myself was okay, as well as necessary for my health and my children; all of my children. As a result, I began to find myself again and not only focus on my emotional health, but to take time for my physical health and total wellbeing. It wasn't easy and the progress has been slow. I found I had to be patient and self-forgiving, if my life was going to change and remain changed. Luckily, I acquired tools that helped me from becoming too overwhelmed. I also began to understand how I could stay true to myself in the midst of the stress that having an addicted child could bring. Most important of all, I saw myself differently and that made all the difference.

BEWARE THE MINEFIELD

Setting boundaries could be one of the hardest and yet most important lessons we have to learn. Being caretakers by nature, we are programmed to make everyone happy. We want to fix what we see broken by trying to take control of it. But dealing with our addict children frequently finds us losing that control—something we never really had in the first place.

At first, we justify our compromises until manipulation and disrespect become normal. Too often, the main reason for this is we neglected to put on our own oxygen masks first before trying to save our children. Without setting clear limitations, our lives will be full of disarray and uncertainty—and happiness will elude us.

Cheri's Story

Until addiction cursed my family, I never realized how important boundaries were or how much those boundaries have changed.

Generations ago, children learned about boundaries early in life. There was no question regarding right and wrong. If you did something wrong, it was almost certain your parents would side with the neighbor, teacher or family member who cited your wrongdoing. Individuals born in those generations would not think to question authority. Boundaries were clear and so were the consequences for violating those boundaries. There was a feeling of security in clearly knowing what was expected.

But with each generation, boundaries have become less clear, respect for authority less important, and parents have stopped siding with teachers and others. Today, it seems there is a new ideology where boundaries, if they exist at all, constantly change. In this new society, children seem to head the household, teachers have no authority and employees tell their employers what they will and will not do. The result of these changes is chaos and confusion. Like a minefield, we don't know where or when explosions will happen. Violence seems to be everywhere. The world is just not the same anymore.

A wise man once said, "God does not put boundaries in place to punish us. He puts them in place to keep us safe." So it is in life. Fences, railroad warning signs and speed limits are established for our safety, as is identification to pick children up from school. There are locks and alarms to protect our homes and there are security gates and procedures at airports.

Boundaries and addiction also go hand-in-hand and probably are the most difficult to determine. I discovered that firsthand as I continue my struggle to establish clear-cut, non-negotiable limits with my addict child. Setting defined limitations is often the most challenging because many of us were brought up in homes with blurred boundaries, especially those who came from families where addiction was already present.

Cheri's Parable

It was a bright, sunny, spring day. A gentle breeze softly blew and the air was filled with anticipation; flowers blooming, birds were singing, gentle rains and the laughter of children happy to be free after the long winter. With her heart full of joy, she ran down the porch steps, anxious to enjoy the beauty of everything around her. She meandered across the lawn, taking time to stop and smell the flowers along the way. Marveling at their bright yellow, pink and lavender, she continued on her way. The path she took was well worn for she had traveled it many times before, through the woods, over the hill, past the meadow to the small, bubbling brook just before the fence that separated her life from that of the neighbor. She inhaled the fresh air as she walked along the old familiar pathway.

There was no fear as she approached the darker part of the woods just on the other side of the meadow for she had been here many times before. Oh, how many days she had enjoyed reaching that opening where the grass grew thick and lush, and the quiet stillness was rarely disturbed except for the occasional rabbit or deer. Often, on her way to the brook, she would stop and rest, read a book, or just revel in the tranquility. It was a quiet place where time seemed to stand still.

Today, however, the path seemed to be taking a little longer. It was difficult to find the meadow. The shady spots that scared her a little because they almost completely blocked the sun, making strange shadows, seemed to go on forever. But that did not deter her for she knew it was just a little further along. Finally, she reached the meadow where she stopped to fully enjoy the open space and sunshine, especially since the darker part of the path had seemed to be so long. She then continued toward the brook. She loved the sound of the water as it cascaded over the rocks and pebbles in its path. She never tired of feeling the cool water as it slid over her tired feet. Sometimes, her childhood would return and she'd find herself splashing and giggling like a young schoolgirl. But it seemed those days were becoming fewer and farther between.

Unexpected Heroes

Feeling adventurous, she wanted to continue a little further. It had been years since she had seen the old fence line and she was curious to see how it was holding up. She remembered the fence had seemed a little ragged the last time she had been there. It had made her sad; feeling like the fence deserved more care. Her mother had told her to stay away from the fence. She warned her that just on the other side things were not as lovely as they were in her own backyard. But today she couldn't deny her curiosity. She just had to know. After all, she reasoned, she was older now. She knew how to take care of herself.

Carefully, she stepped over the fence and was surprised at how sturdy it actually was after all. It gave her comfort to know that the fence had safely protected her for so long. Curious, she wandered a little farther. Things really were different on this side and part of her became angry her mother had forbidden her the freedom to explore and enjoy this beautiful piece of the world. The further into the woods she went, the more excited she became. There were so many new and exciting things to see, feel, smell and touch. It was as if her senses became truly alive for the first time in her life. She wasn't sure how much time had passed and wondered if she should head back, but her adventurous side pressed her onward.

After walking and exploring for a while, off in the distance, she could hear the sound of water. Her steps quickened and she hurried along, anxious to experience everything before she turned back for home. As she neared the water, the sound became louder. Upon topping the next hill, she spotted it immediately—the loveliest waterfall she had ever seen. She was struck by the power it held. The water rushed over the rocks and down small hills. It splashed on the banks and grabbed leaves and bark, pulling them into the current with strength and power she had never seen in her small brook. Throwing caution to the wind, she wanted to experience the rush of the water for herself. Clamoring down the bank, she jumped in and found herself caught in the strong current.

At first she was thrilled with the excitement of letting the water move her along. But, after a little while, she began to tire. She wanted out of the water but it had a firm grip on her. She found herself being tossed through some rapids and cut her hands, feet and knees on the jagged rocks, as she clutched at everything in her reach, trying desperately to be freed from the current. The water became deeper and her head kept being pulled under the now threatening stream.

Her excitement was gone and she could only think of getting out of the water and heading back to the safety on the other side of the fence. Just as she was losing hope, she saw a large branch hanging over the edge of the bank. If I can just grab hold of that, I can get out of here, she thought. Then she fought with all her might. Finally, as she felt her strength beginning to wane, she was able to grab the branch and pull herself free.

Thankful to be safely out of the rushing current, she rested on the bank, trying to catch her breath and remember why she thought the rushing water looked more inviting than her own peaceful, little brook. After a time, she rose to her feet and began her journey back. However, there was no safe path on this side of the fence and she was uncertain of her direction. The sun was beginning to go down and her anxiety was rising. Moving toward where she thought she had come from, she looked for landmarks.

She began to run, anxious to be home before the sun went down. Running and stumbling she made her way. Her hands and feet hurt from being cut in the rapids, her knees now more sore after falling so many times, tripping over roots and branches she didn't realize were in her way. The woods were appearing more and more frightening as time passed. It was getting darker and the slight path was harder to see. The tears that pooled in her eyes and ran down her cheeks were of no help in seeing where she was headed. She wanted to stop and rest but darkness was closing in.

Alone, injured, frightened and lost, she finally dropped to the ground, exhausted. She was sure she should have reached the fence by now. Rising, again, she continued along in the darkness, feeling her way and hoping she would find the fence soon. Stumbling, falling, getting up and moving forward, she continued onward until she realized the fence was nowhere to be found. Reaching the end of her strength, she found a small shelter in the brush and slept.

The next morning, she awakened in a state of despair. Had she been walking in circles? Had she stumbled into the wrong part of the woods? How would she ever find her way back? The fence had always been there. She had always known she was safe as long as the fence was there and she didn't cross it. But she couldn't find the fence. Her sense of direction was gone. Her "safety net" had failed. Who moved the fence? For, surely, that is what must have happened. Yet, she knew she must find her way home, so she journeyed on.

Finally, she heard it…the faint sound of someone calling her name in the distance. Mother. Just the sound of her voice brought hope that she could find her way back. Then she heard other voices of family members and friends. While she had stumbled around, lost on the wrong side of the fence, they had been calling for her, trying to let her know they were there.

As she walked, the voices grew nearer. She emerged from the woods and saw the faces of those who loved her. And there, standing faithful as ever, was the sturdy old fence. Grateful for her loved ones and the safety of the fence, she rejoiced upon reaching them. Even so, the moment she reached the fence, she looked back, thinking about the rush of the waterfall, the thrill of losing control to it and the beauty it possessed. And even though it had frightened her, she was sure she could conquer it. As the fear began to give way to fond memories, she contemplated going back, just for a little while, just to have one more look. Just one.

HELD HOSTAGE

Laura's Story

I 'll never forget what the police officer told me that night, even though many of the details aren't clear anymore. I remember there was a light rain that fell after we went to bed so by the time I was jolted awake by the phone, the streets reflected different colors. I remember thinking; of course these things never happen in the middle of the day. And I remember the story the officer who found our daughter and our car, shared with us.

Reporting our car stolen, after she failed to return it when requested, was probably one of the hardest things I ever had to do. After years of experience, we could see the signs in recent weeks as things had begun to spiral out of control with our daughter. Like most addicts' families, we knew that roller coaster, as we navigated between periods of hope and despair. But the stakes became much higher when our grandson was born and we realized her actions, as well as ours, not only directly affected her but also her child.

By the time we arrived at the deserted gas station where the car was parked on the side, our daughter had already been arrested and taken away. After confirming the car was ours, we were asked by one of the police officers that met us there, if we were willing to make a statement regarding the circumstances leading up to the theft. Since the car was in my name only, I would have to be the one who made the statement. I agreed that I would.

The officer seemed unusually tired and especially compassionate towards us. He shook his head and quietly said, "It's a real problem, meth." We agreed and I responded by saying he must see this kind of thing all the time. He nodded. He then shared something he had experienced just a few days before that had really driven home for him the horror families of addicts face.

He told us he had been called to the home of a family whose son was threatening the safety of his parents, and they had finally called the police for help. Upon entering the home, which the officer described as "really nice at one time," he found the place to be completely trashed and the parents to be holed up in their bedroom. They were essentially trapped there, as their son and his friends had completely taken over the rest of the house.

These parents, out of fear, never left that room except to leave the house and return again only to that room. They were able to use a separate entrance that let them come and go without entering the rest of the house. They reported their son and his friends had threatened them, and they were no longer allowed to enter the rest of their home. So out of fear, they stayed only in that one bedroom. Their home had been completely taken over. When I asked how they were eating, if they never went into their own kitchen, he commented on the fast food wrappers he had seen lying around.

When the officer asked those parents why they didn't just set boundaries and tell their son to leave, they had no answer for him. He told me he had never seen anything like it. And of course, since their son and his friends weren't present when the police arrived, there was really nothing they could do in spite of the evidence of drug use seen throughout the house.

He strongly advised the parents of ways they could regain control of their home by changing the locks, etc. and then calling the police, again, when their son returned. But he knew they probably wouldn't. He told me what he had seen that day was the worst example of enabling he has ever experienced in his entire career.

We had provided the car our daughter was driving primarily as a means for her to have transportation back and forth to work. She seemed to be making good decisions and also appeared to be excelling at her job. We became so hopeful that things were finally turning around for her. After all, she couldn't work if she had no way to get there, right? Plus, riding the bus took much longer and the sooner she could return home from work each day, the sooner she could be there to take care of her son.

But readily available transportation served only to enable her. The realization we had contributed to this—again—made us feel even more helpless as we watched things unravel before our eyes. Even though we warned her, I felt horrible calling to report the car stolen. I had to fight hard to maintain my composure because it was difficult to see as the tears filled my eyes. I filled out the paperwork and signed it, stating I was willing to prosecute. I couldn't believe it had come to this. I was calling my own daughter—my sweetest baby—a criminal.

I shared some of my anguish with the officer and he assured me we had done the right thing. He explained while she probably wouldn't be charged, since it was a family vehicle, versus a deliberate theft of a random car; our actions were still setting boundaries. He encouraged us to stay firm and stand by those boundaries for our own protection as well as in the best interest of our daughter. He commented again he would never forget those hostage parents and I didn't miss that his tone seemed to be a subtle warning. I knew I would never forget them either.

SECURING THE BORDER

One boundary that can weigh heavily and carries much torment concerns protecting our grandchildren, even at the expense of our addict children's feelings. It is a difficult decision to determine whether the addict parent should see his or her children if still using drugs.

Some grandparents are afraid to halt visits out of fear of retaliation by the addict, guilt of breaking the parent/child bond or simply feel it is the only way to unconditionally love their addict child. But the addict parent frequently cannot be counted on, and often they are either late for visits or don't show up at all. If the addict parent arrives strung out, hyper or nodding off, there's no one present, anyhow. Their young children can sense this, resulting in feelings they don't know how to process.

We are in a precarious position, but conditions must be set for our addict and even our addict in recovery, if behaviors are still volatile and have not changed. The grandchildren we're raising must be protected so they feel safe and secure.

Lynne's Story

While we cared for our grandson, his mother tried to get sober in a sober living house. We assumed when a person goes into sober living, he or she is required to remain sober or else is asked to leave. But that's not always the case. Sometimes when randomly tested, the addict uses someone else's urine or another remedy to avoid being caught, even though clearly using.

Our daughter's first week in sober living seemed to go well. She looked clear and was actually smiling, again. But it didn't take long for me to see she was back to using.

She often arrived late to our weekly scheduled visits with our grandson and wasn't looking well. By our third visit, her skin looked pasty with that awful metallic "meth" odor seeping through her pores. Even Brady, who had been so excited to see her, felt something was wrong—you could see it on his face. Instead of sitting close to our daughter, he preferred to sit closer to me while he tightly held onto my neck.

I could no longer ignore what my gut was telling me and I questioned her. She got angry and her temper flared. "Don't be ridiculous," she answered. "I am not using and it's none of your business why I'm late!" I was shocked at her outburst but it rang familiar. Every word out of her mouth validated what I was thinking. But how would I find out for sure? If she was fooling the sober living house, how could I get accurate data? I had a baby to protect. What if she took her anger out on him or made a poor judgment call while playing with him and he got hurt on one of their play dates? He was already visibly upset every time she arrived late and had tantrums for days when she left. It was not fair to him.

When she arrived at our next play date, almost forty minutes late and looking worse than before, my husband and I knew it was time to do something. We met with our daughter alone and told her we knew she was using and it wasn't healthy for her to be near a baby with drugs in her system. We shared with her how upset Brady was when she didn't show up on time. We told her it wasn't okay for her to come in and out of his life like a revolving door. We then explained how we were trying our hardest to give her baby a stable life and inconsistency would only serve to tear down that foundation. I thought she would yell at us at that point, but she didn't. Deep down, I believe she understood she couldn't be a part of his life until she was healthy. We said we loved her, though we needed to curtail her visits, and she left.

Even though she seemed to accept our terms, she also seemed to forget them and would ask when she could see him every time she called. I repeated she could when she was clean and in a huff, she'd hang up on me. Not trusting my daughter on drugs, I also began to use the alarm in the house. It was exhausting but we kept reminding ourselves to hold true to do what was best for the baby.

We knew how hard this was on our daughter. So without Brady, we'd meet with her at various coffee shops to share stories about her son and show her photographs. Still, there was no change. She couldn't stop using.

It was a difficult but necessary decision and I will always stand by the boundaries my husband and I set for the sake of this child. It proved to be sound judgment. He's growing up feeling protected, loved and cared for in the healthiest way possible. He knew his bio mother had a disease and could not take care of him and is fortunate we could.

OBSTACLES AHEAD

Addiction is called a "family disease" because every family member is affected. An addict in the family takes everything from us emotionally, and happy times are often replaced by an obsession to stop the addict's damaging behavior.

As parents, we become so consumed with stress and worry we don't even realize how much potential damage is being inflicted on the addict's siblings. Without intention, our other children are often put on the back burner because they may seem to be okay. But they are not. They have a front row seat as they watch their parents become totally engulfed in a painful and negative situation and often don't understand why the bad kid in the family is getting all the attention. And if that's not insult enough, the bad kid's child is also now in the picture. Consequently, resentment frequently builds. As siblings reach adulthood, this discord may increase, causing more hurt and possible irreversible damage.

And it doesn't stop there. While we are raising the children of our addict children, we also have other grandchildren who need our love and attention. Because we are putting all our time and effort into the grandchild or grandchildren we're personally raising, this can leave little energy for the other grandchildren who may feel cheated and left out.

It's not easy and it's not fair. We see our other grandchildren, many with blissfully normal lives with two biological parents; and we are grateful. We just wish the grandchild we are rearing could also have that life. Consequently, we try to bring a sense of normalcy and balance into the lives of the grandchildren we're raising. All the while, fully knowing our very best efforts can never completely replace what should have been.

Betty's Story

My family is complicated. Our family dynamics are so convoluted, sometimes I feel like it's all I can do to just hang on. As I raise my addict daughter's son, I have another daughter who is successful in every facet of her life and has two sons of her own. My grandson is jealous of his cousins because of what they have that he doesn't—a mom and a dad, a nice house and after school activities that are a struggle for me to afford. I try to make it up to my grandson by going above and beyond as much as I can and yet I don't spend as much time spoiling my other two grandsons, as I would like. Truth be known, I just want to be a regular grandma to all three of my grandsons, instead of being grandma to two of them and grandma/mom to one. I don't feel like it's fair to any of them or to me.

For years, my "good" daughter suffered while we were busy dealing with our "bad" daughter. I wasn't able to go to many of her activities because I was too busy taking her sister to court or drug counseling or whatever. Now, she sees that her own children don't get as much attention from me because I am raising her sister's kid. The balancing act is exhausting. I have been doing this for years.

The highs and lows just wear me out. I try my best to get to every activity my other grandsons have so they can feel my presence and support, but also so my daughter never feels slighted.

However, there are times when I just can't do it and have no choice but to tell her how sorry I was I couldn't make it. Even though I can see her trying to understand, I'm sure deep down; it hurts her as much as it does me. I know this adds to the resentment she already feels for all the years of lost time she endured as a result of her sister's addiction. It is a deep-rooted angst that never completely goes away for either of us.

We are both slowly coming to a better place in our lives with regards to the pain of the past but these things take time. The sad thing is we have no choice but to ride the rollercoaster of emotions for now. The children can't wait for us to work through things.

My greatest hope is my daughter can just take my hand and walk with me while I do the very best I can to fulfill both my roles now as a parent and grandparent. Some days this is much easier to do than others.

DISSENTION IN THE RANKS

Teresa's Story

This is the story of three women—my two daughters and me. Ann and Liz are only fifteen months apart, now ages thirty-two and thirty-three. We were always a team of three. Their father left when they were just four and five years old and never looked back.

As both daughters will undoubtedly attest, my constant mantra when they were growing up was "sisters always stick together"—and for the most part they did. I honestly felt I raised them the same, even though they became two very different women.

Both were rebellious in high school and partners in crime—a difficult time for me. However, after high school, Ann, my youngest, settled down and began building a healthy adult life. As a single mom, she received both her Bachelor's and Master's degrees while working full time. She still coaches Little League and is actively involved in her children's education. She continues to move up the corporate ladder in her job and just purchased her own home after years of saving. If you "Googled" the word "responsible," you just might see her face.

My eldest daughter, Liz, on the other hand, got pregnant at sixteen and dropped out of high school (but later got her diploma).

I know now that she began using drugs in her early teens, crushing and snorting her prescribed ADD medicine, Ritalin. The drug use escalated right under my nose—marijuana, uppers, downers, hallucinogens, pain pills and eventually, heroin. Due to all the red flags, I had her in counseling from the time she was small. But she quickly became out of control and has been most of her adult life.

Of the two girls, Liz was probably the kinder and more sensitive. However, she was also the more depressed, lonely and impulsive. By the time she was twenty-four, she had three children and always chose boyfriends who treated her poorly. While I have no doubt she loved her children with her entire being, she had a disease that was stronger than love.

The stories I've heard from her children have shocked, angered and saddened me. Her first-born son, now eighteen, had his bedroom used to grow marijuana (complete with grow lights, seeds and harvest). The twelve-year-old has seen needles in the apartment (supposedly used for allergies). Her seven-year-old recently shared he peed in cups for mommy (so she could pass drug tests). She's been in and out of detox, rehab, jail, monitored probation and intensive outpatient programs.

Finally, things got so bad I couldn't ignore them and had to step in. Her children came to me for a weekend visit and I never returned them. Fortunately or maybe unfortunately, Liz was nowhere to be found. I was told she and her husband were evicted from their apartment and either living in her car or on friends' couches. No one knew how to reach them. In effect, the children were abandoned and I was able to get emergency guardianship. I then received full legal guardianship and the three children have been with me ever since.

Her sister, Ann has told me many times she received no attention growing up because, even though she was the younger sister, she was always the "responsible" one. I'll never forget the time she asked me, "So if I quit my job and do drugs—you'll pay attention to me?"

She also likes to remind me her children do not have a grandma because I must now raise Liz's kids and have no time for them. Meanwhile, I am trying to be all things to all people and feel I'm being stretched beyond the breaking point. But surprisingly, I'm still standing.

All Ann can see is the hurt and anguish Liz has caused her children, our family and me. She sees what Liz's many years of drug use have done to my plans for the future. I am sixty years old, raising three children and the youngest is four years old. She knows I have been robbed of every valuable I've owned. She sees the horrific circumstances in which Liz's children have lived. She has no empathy or compassion for her sister. Any trust or kindness she previously felt has been replaced with suspicion, betrayal and resentment.

What Ann doesn't understand, however, is I truly believe Liz did not choose to be an addict. She did not intend to abandon her children or to become a liar, thief or person willing to do almost anything to get high. I feel she has an illness more powerful than she is. But Ann can no longer even pretend to care for her sister. She has cut off all ties to her. She will not tolerate any attempts I have made to bring them back together and hangs up the phone if I even mention Liz's name.

Just as Ann doesn't understand Liz—Liz doesn't understand how her sister could abandon her. She is devastated by how her sister seems to hate her. Liz has called, texted and emailed her sister, begging for her sister's forgiveness and understanding. Ann will not respond.

Currently, Liz is in rehab and soon Ann will be getting married. When she first got engaged, Liz was to be her sister's maid of honor (as Ann was at Liz's marriage). Because she was in rehab, Ann asked another person to fill in this role. Over time, Liz was demoted to bridesmaid and later excluded from the wedding party altogether. About six months ago, Ann decided she did not even want her sister in attendance. She had concerns. What if she showed up high? What if she didn't show? What if she brought her addict husband? Who would pay for her dress and other expenses?

I would have. I have forgiven Liz, as only a mother can. Her sister has not. The situation worsened a few months ago. Ann forbade me from even mentioning her sister to her. "She's not invited and I'm not changing my mind," she said. Determined, I made a final appeal to Ann to please allow her sister to attend. But it backfired. I was not only "uninvited" as well, but my own daughter cut off ties with me.

My grandchildren know Liz is no longer welcome and it bothers these children who are caught in the middle of something they don't understand. So now we have an immature daughter who wants her life neat and drama-free, a broken addicted daughter and a mother trying to fix everything and everyone. This is quite a threesome and not at all how we began. I feel so heartbroken.

The wedding is in two weeks. Ann and I have gradually started communicating. But sadly, I have not been involved in any of the planning for the wedding. I can't seem to let go of the hurt I carry and what I know Liz feels. I don't understand how one sister can be so cold to her sister's needs. It also devastates me to see Liz continue to choose drugs without regard to her own children. I am so torn. Nevertheless, I love my daughters and wish them nothing but health, happiness and love.

Unexpected Heroes

I realize I can't be the one to bring them back together. Only they can do that. But that doesn't alleviate my sadness. I don't know how this story will end. I can only pray that such a thing as "happily ever after" really does exist. I know I will never stop looking for it.

HONOR THE FALLEN

How does a parent face the loss of a child? There truly is no greater pain regardless of the circumstances leading up to their death. A mother should never have to bury her child. The loss never leaves our hearts. We miss them beyond words. It is the worst kind of pain a parent can endure. The second most difficult pain is telling their child.

Julie's Story

The endless flow of visitors and family had slowed. Despite all efforts to have someone more qualified than I deliver the news before someone slipped and said something; the time had come. Dread filled me and drained my already taxed body. With the support of my momma and daddy, I called out, "Kyler, come here honey—Mimi needs to talk to you."

Bounding into the kitchen, holding a miniature toy car, he said, "Yes Mimi?" I patted my lap, and he obligingly crawled up in it. Sweaty from playing outside, and smelling a lot like a dirty little puppy, he sat there fidgeting—playing with the little car in his hands. My parents watched on silently, fighting back their own tears, as I chose my words carefully. I had to make them age appropriate. I had to deliver news I knew would break his heart. I was at such a loss. "How do I do this, God? Tell me. How do I do this?"

At that moment a little voice said, "Mimi—what's wrong?"

I could wait no longer.

"I need to tell you something, Kyler."

"Yeah?" He responded

I choked but continued. "Your momma isn't in jail anymore. She's in heaven."

There was a long silence. It seemed like an eternity. I could almost see the thoughts turning in his little four-year-old mind. Chunky little legs swinging, head tucked down and dirty little fingers turning the wheels on his little toy car, he turned around and looked at me and said, "You mean my momma is dead?"

"Yes," I replied.

"Will I get to see her again?" he asked.

"Yes. We will go to see her in a little while."

He sat there in silence, still pondering what I had told him.

I asked, "Do you need to ask me any questions?"

He replied, "Not right now, Mimi. Can I go play now?"

"Yes. You can go play."

As soon as he rounded the corner I began to sob, and expressed a fear all of us raising addict's children have asked, "What if I screw him up too?"

That's what drugs can do—crush lives, futures and families and leave behind only the guilt, anger and what-ifs. It's just so terrible. You have so many hopes and dreams for your kids and you want them to be able to accomplish all you couldn't do. You love them before you have them, and then when you watch them throw their lives away, there's nothing you can do.

As a parent—a single parent—I did everything I knew to save my rebellious child. As soon as I discovered my daughter was smoking pot and using paint thinner to get high at the tender age of twelve, I used tough love and got her into a boot camp.

When Emily was home, she kept trying to leave the house so often I slept on the couch to keep her from sneaking out at night. I even changed jobs with hours that would allow me to get home when she did. But still she ran away. That's when I worked with local law enforcement, got her into another tough-love boot camp and had her put on probation.

After that, thinking it might help, Emily went to live with her grandparents for a year. But it made no difference and made me sick when she reunited with her boyfriend, a drug supplier, and got pregnant right away. She was just sixteen. I'd desperately hoped having a baby would change her ways, but that didn't work. She just kept slipping through the cracks. Still, I hoped and prayed and hoped some more.

On the night of Emily's death, I was at the kitchen window when I saw the sheriff and his wife, who was a deputy, along with her boss and his wife get out of a police car. If I'd known the news they were going to deliver, I would have run out the back door and kept running. But I thought perhaps my daughter, who was so skilled at running away, had escaped from jail.

When she was first arrested, only a day ago, I got the call to come pick up my grandson at her house and bring him to mine. He was too little to understand much. But when I put him in the car seat in the back, he was sobbing. My daughter had asked me to leave with him before they put her into the sheriff's car so he wouldn't have to see that. But I watched from my rear view mirror.

My grandson was still crying. I asked him why he was so upset as he'd stayed with me often. His answer broke my heart. "Where am I going to live?" With everything he'd just seen happen, his main concern was where he was going to live. As wounded, ignored, neglected and abused as he was...all he wanted was some love and some stability.

I told him, "Honey, you're going to live with me."

"Forever?" he asked.

And I immediately replied, "Yes"—not realizing it would be true.

Before the sheriff and his entourage could even make their way up the walkway to knock on the door of my house, I quickly opened it. "Where is she?"' I yelled. They quietly came in and told me four hours earlier Emily took a bed sheet, tied it above a partition between the toilet and cot of the county jail, and hung herself. She was only twenty years old and it was her brother Colton's birthday. When they told me Emily's body had already been taken to the morgue for an autopsy—it hit me.

They'd won. The drugs had won. Methamphetamine had another victim. A once smart vivacious girl with the looks of a model had taken her own life. The drug culture, the twenty-pound weight loss, the excuse-making, the sorry friends, the broken taillight that led to her and her boyfriend's arrest the day before, all came spiraling down in a drug-fueled haze of despondency and disappointment and a bed sheet.

It's been ten years since I lost my precious Emily. My grandson just turned fourteen. He is such a good kid, and has every reason not to be. Orphaned by his mother's suicide at age four and his biological father's voluntary termination of rights, his life might have taken a turn for the worse.

But today my grandson is working on his Eagle Scout requirements—something that would have never happened for him had he been left in an addicted, dysfunctional home. I feel blessed he's in my life and even more blessed I was given the opportunity to change someone's life. Ironically, I know that due to my daughter's death, I have been given a gift. I am free to raise him completely free from any stress or pressure from the drug world.

That being said, like any mother and with all of my heart, I would have gladly returned that gift in exchange for her life. I could never have made the choice between her and my grandson. I am grateful I didn't have to.

GONE

Lynne's Story

A t the Philadelphia Airport, I was waiting with my husband and our five-year-old grandson for our flight back home to Los Angeles when my cell phone rang. I didn't recognize the number and almost didn't answer. It was a young woman's voice. She said her name was Lindsay and was calling from the drug rehab where my daughter was being treated. Why was she calling *me*? Didn't she know I hadn't spoken to Jaime in months?

Jaime's incarceration, her stay in rehab and our taking over the parenting of her son threw me into a tailspin. The last thing I wanted was to talk about my daughter. Our hands were full. Stu and I had been there to help parent Brady since his birth and took over full-time when Jaime began using, again. It was a constant struggle acting as parents while Jaime, no longer in our house, attempted to parent from afar whenever the impulse hit. Going to jail and then court-ordered rehab, she was forced to get sober. But after ten years, in and out of drug use, we still feared it wouldn't stick.

"I'm so sorry, Lindsay," I swiftly answered. "Right now I have very little to do with my daughter. If Jaime needs something, could you please call her sister, Tracy?" Lindsay said she was aware we hadn't had much contact, but Jaime had an accident in the

215

bathroom and she wanted to give me the number of a woman to call at the hospital.

Oh, God. What now? Instead of feeling compassion for my adult daughter, all I felt was bitterness. What a burden she's been. We're at the airport, for God's sake. Jaime's probably requesting I come see her or bring her a nightgown or some random personal item. Jaime certainly could have had the nurse call Tracy for those items. But my daughter, famous for using the guilt card, most likely figured this was one way she might convince us to come see her.

I asked Stu to take Brady for a snack, that I needed to make a phone call and would fill him in later. After finding a quieter place to sit in the airport, I dialed the number I was given. The woman—I assumed was a hospital nurse—politely explained Jaime had passed out in the shower, cut her chin and was brought to the hospital that morning by the paramedics.

"Please forgive me," I interrupted, "but we're on the east coast at the airport so there's nothing I can help you with." I know I must have sounded hard and uncaring but I was so tired of all the years of addiction, manipulation and drama and was almost relieved we were out of town. I just wanted some peace.

"I must apologize," the woman said. Then she paused. "Because you're out of state, I have to tell you what has happened."

Just as she was about to continue, a flurry of people entered the airport gate where I was sitting. The woman was very soft-spoken and it was getting noisy. I asked her to hold on a moment while I moved to a different location so I could hear her better. Luckily, I found another gate where no one was sitting and got back on the phone. The woman resumed speaking.

"The paramedics informed me after they picked your daughter up, she kept passing out in the ambulance."

"It could be drugs," I interjected. "My daughter's been in a court-ordered rehab and she might have relapsed. I haven't seen her in several months."

"I'll make a note of that," the woman responded. "Since you're out of state, it's my obligation to give you this information."

There was an uneasy silence. I could barely make out what she was saying. Her words seemed muffled.

"We did everything we could," the woman quietly said, "but we couldn't revive her."

What? What is she saying? I felt like my sense of hearing kept breaking up, as if I was going under water and out, again.

"She expired at eight thirty this morning," the woman apologetically said.

I began to shake uncontrollably.

"What? What did you say? Are you saying she's…gone?"

I could hardly speak through my trembling and my tears. People began trickling into the gate area where I was sitting, so I cowered into a corner, cradling the phone tightly to my ear. "How?" I managed to ask—my voice cracked.

She said she didn't know. Because Jaime was alive when she arrived at the hospital, an autopsy would need to be performed to determine the cause of death.

"I'm a nun," she caringly said. "I'll stay on the phone for as long as you need me."

People in the airport were staring at me and I couldn't stop crying. Holding the phone to my chest, I was trying to process all of this. "I can't believe it, I can't believe it!" I kept repeating out loud, while trying not to draw attention to myself. *She can't be gone…she's gone?*

Trying to compose myself, I put the phone back up to my ear, thanked the nun and told her I needed to call my children and find my husband. "I'll be all right," I told her. She said to please call her when we got home. I hung up and called my youngest son, Josh. He could hardly understand me through my hysteria. Because of all of Stu's heart issues, he logically thought something happened to his dad. Josh was in shock. But I think he said he'd call his siblings, Tracy and Adam, or else I did. I can't remember...

I worked my way to our gate where I found Stu and Brady. My husband took one look at me and knew something was very wrong. Brady was on the floor playing with his toy cars. Fortunately, I could pull Stu aside without Brady noticing. When I broke the news to him, Stu didn't get emotional. He said he wasn't shocked or surprised—just terribly sad.

How I sat on a plane for three thousand miles, I'll never know. My daughter was gone.

Brady was looking at me, confused. "Why are you crying, Mommy?" he asked.

Stu replied Jaime was very sick and mom was upset. We'd explain to Brady what really happened to Jaime when we got home. I was numb. But now it was real. We were mommy and daddy in the truest sense—grandparents raising our grandchild.

When our plane finally landed in Los Angeles from Philadelphia, I was wiped out. I still couldn't fathom my daughter was gone.

Stu got the luggage from the carousel and we took a taxi from the airport to our house. The ride seemed to take forever. After bringing in the suitcases, we sat Brady down on the staircase, our favorite spot to talk, and quietly explained to him that Jaime was with God. We said because she took drugs, it hurt her body so much it wouldn't work anymore and she died. He seemed to accept our words but I'm not sure how much he understood about a person dying or the impact her death would have on his life. She hadn't been his mother during the formative years, but we were sure he remembered a "sense" of her. We reassured him we would always be his mom and dad, would be there for him and would answer every question he had, in the best way possible.

With that, we certainly weren't expecting the question we were about to be asked. We had just arrived at the cemetery for our daughter's burial. I was in a daze and felt nauseous knowing my daughter was in a casket next to us. It was surreal. We eerily walked to the gravesite, as the pallbearers carried the casket. Brady had been anxious during the car ride but was now very quiet as he walked beside me. When I looked down at him, it was then I realized that I not only just lost my daughter but this poor little boy had just lost his birth mother. What could be going through his head? I forced myself to come out of my own grief to lovingly ask him if he was okay and if he had any questions.

"I really want to see her," he said.

My heart stopped. How was I going to handle this? She was sealed in a pine box.

Thinking he might be distraught, grasping at straws, I asked, "Brady, why do you want to see her?"

"Because," he answered, I want to see if she looks like this…"

At that moment, he scrunched up his face in a contorted fashion and stuck his tongue out the side of his mouth.

I almost lost it and had to cup my mouth to hold back my laughter.

He then added with great seriousness, "In a movie I saw once, animals died and looked like that. I wanted to see if that was how she looked."

It was so good this little boy was thinking like a child and good for Stu and I to have a little bit of comic relief. But we had to answer his question.

Stu assured him this kind of thing only happened to animals, while I remained poised ready to give him my answer.

"Brady," I softly said, "Jaime is at peace now. Her face is relaxed and very beautiful because she's with God."

He grabbed my hand and Stu's, and then he smiled. But it was Brady who helped us smile that difficult day and still keeps us smiling, even when we least expect it.

VI

BEACON OF HOPE

"We can't all be heroes because somebody has
to sit on the curb and clap as they go by."

—*WILL ROGERS*

WORDS OF GLORY

The gift of laughter is precious. Like gentle touches and hugs, it's essential in order for life to thrive in the best way possible. It is a powerful organic antidote to combat stress, pain and conflict. It helps to relax your body, releases endorphins, improves your immune system and protects your heart. It's no wonder the phrase "Laughter is the Best Medicine" is used so often.

With our new lives raising grandchildren, many of us never expected we'd receive wonderful gifts of laughter along with this new responsibility. Most of these unsolicited gifts surprise us and sometimes leave us in awe as they come in the form of pearls of joy and wisdom. Out of the mouths of babes...

Resourceful Kids

My grandson was playing tee ball when he had to go to the bathroom. His coach had told the boys to never leave their bases during a game. So what did he do? He picked up the base and took it with him.

My four-year-old grandson/son loved his little wooden toy trains. Lately, every time we went to the train store, he changed his tune and begged me to buy him an electric train. On our last visit to the store, I was relieved to have a good excuse. On the train box, it stated: "For eight years old and up." When I told him, he looked at me seriously and said, "Mom, even though it's for eight-year-olds, the box won't know I'm only four!" *Foiled again!*

Our three-year-old grandson was asking for a donut. He pointed to the box on the kitchen counter and said, "I want one of those." My husband, in the other room couldn't see what he was pointing to and asked him what he wanted. Not wanting to draw attention to anything, I responded, "He wants a d-o-n-u-t" thinking he wouldn't know what I was talking about if I spelled it out. Not missing a beat, our grandson marched over to my husband and said, "Please may I have a d-o-n-u-t?" He got one.

My grandson was happily reading his favorite book aloud to himself, while our dog sat at his feet. That's when I noticed it was upside down. Trying to be helpful, I reached over to turn it around and said, "You can't read that way. The book is upside down!" Irritated, he immediately responded, "I'm reading to the dog!"

At preschool, my grandson was watching all the young moms of his friends strolling in with babies in carriages.

"Mom," he said pleadingly, "I really want a little baby sister."

How will I get out of this one? I'm in my late fifties.

"Having a baby sister would take all the time away from you," I explained, trying to be creative. "If she cried, I'd have to tend to her needs first."

He quietly listened and seemed to be pondering what I was saying.

"She'd play with all your toys," I added, "and might even break them."

He continued to listen.

"Having a baby sister just might not be the greatest," I concluded.

"Okay," he said, as if he accepted my argument. "Then I'll have a baby brother."

My young grandson was amusing himself with a small ball I had just purchased for him and said, "I climbed under your legs to get that ball." I answered, "I know. You almost knocked me over!" He proudly responded, "Ya, it took me *years* to learn how to do that!"

Barely four years old, my granddaughter asked for a tablet so she could write on it. I looked over and in minutes she had used about forty pages. I told her not to use up all the paper and her response was, "But, Nanny, I am writing a book!"

I caught my granddaughter eating sugar straight out of the sugar canister. I told her we don't eat out of canisters and she responded, "Okay, will you put some in a bowl, please?"

Almost four-year-old wisdom: "When I get hurt, God will glue me back together and put me down to dry."

⟨⟩

Loving Kids

I was strapping my grandson into his car seat when he looked up at me through his long eyelashes and said, "I love you. Do you want to be my friend?" I was charmed and responded, "Forever, I love you too!" And then he asked, "Do you want to smell my stinky shoes?"

Random discussion in the car: "You know, Nana, you could kiss me on my nose." I smiled. "I could?" I asked. "Yes, like a butterfly landed on my nose. Then that would be a butterfly kiss!" *Giggles and enough smiles to last all day!*

My beautiful blonde baby doll came up to me this morning, hugged me and said, "Thank you for taking care of me, Grandma."

Unexpected Heroes

On Mother's Day, I received a beautiful hand-made card from my ten-year-old grandson/son. It read: "Mom, I Love You Because… It's hard to say why I love you because no words can describe how special you are to me and special you are to everyone else. I'm going to say just a small part of what you are to me. You are an angel who helps people. When they are hurt, you're a loving person, a caring person and a role model. I wish I could give you the life you deserve."

On Father's Day, my husband pouted as he compared our cards. He got a hand-made card in the shape of a necktie from our grandson/son that read only: "Happy Father's Day, Dad!" *That's it?*

⌣⁀

Observant Kids

One day, I was complaining out loud how hard it was being a mother, especially having to pick up a zillion toy cars and put them away, make lunches every day, cook dinner every night, grocery shop and do laundry. My six-year-old-grandson overheard me, walked into the room and said, "Mom, being a parent is hard work so that being a kid can be easy."

Today, I was cleaning up around the pool and I complained about the mess on the deck made by the birds that sit in the tree above that spot and poop. My grandson, not missing a beat, responded, "That's because they don't have any toilet paper!"

"My eyes are all red," my three-year old grandson complained. "I think I might have an *eye confection*."

Noticing a random tear on my four-year-old grandson's cheek and hoping he hadn't been crying, I said, "What's that tear doing there?" His response? "Oh, I'm just leaking."

My grandson walked in the room, stopped in the hallway, stared at a patch of sunlight on the floor and exclaimed, "I found a rainbow on the ground!" When I asked him how he thought that happened, he said, "When the sunlight stands on the ground it makes a rainbow."

Excited to have a school holiday, my grandson exclaimed, "I don't have to go to school, tomorrow, because it's Veterinarian's Day!"

When I picked my grandson up from school today, he said, "I fell on the playground." I asked, "Did you get hurt?" His answer, "No, I just landed...like an airplane!"

After getting up this morning, my grandson, slipped into a grouchy mood, and so I asked him, "What's wrong with you, buddy?" His answer, "Nothing, I'm just having a bad attitude!"

Upon finding a small spot of dry skin on his big toe, my grandson exclaimed: "Hey, my toe is wearing out!"

"I'm clean now!" my grandson announced after his bath one morning. "You are?" I responded. "Yes," he said. "I'm clean and odor free!"

Confused Kids

Before she could talk, my granddaughter was confused about how she fit into the scheme of things. The book, "Are You my Mommy?" came to mind. She wasn't sure what she was—human or animal! She meowed before she could say momma, she walked on all fours for a brief time, and when she played with her stuffed animals; she would put them in her mouth and shake them like our dog. Now, she hisses at the dog! *What's next?*

To my grandson while watching him play with an LED flashlight: "Do you want to be a doctor when you grow up?" His answer, "Noooo. I want to be a doggie!"

On the way to school, my grandson was singing in the car: "I'm gonna swish you a Merry Christmas and a Happy New Year!" I asked him, "Swish you? Are those the words?" He answered confidently. "Yes." So I asked him, "What does that mean?" His answer: "I don't know." *And neither do I.*

My almost four-year-old grandson singing the ABC Song: "A, B, C, D, E, F, G, H, I, J, K, animal, P!

My grandson, who was looking at my phone this morning and spotted the new fitness app I recently loaded, inquired, "What kind of game is that?"

"It's not a game," I answered. "It measures my steps when I exercise,"

Seeming to be in deep thought, he then asked, "You have to step on your phone?"

Kids Know Best

One morning, while my husband was in the middle of breakfast, our five-year-old grandson, whom we're raising, asked my husband to help him build his train tracks. My husband said he was eating and would help as soon as he finished. Impatiently, our grandson asked him again and again and again. My husband repeated he'd help him when he finished eating. Frustrated, our grandson put his hands on his hips and then threw them in the air and said, "I can't do this myself. I'm not God. I'm not an angel. I'm just a man!"

When I hugged my grandson after getting out of the shower, he stated, "I don't like wet hair! I only like wet stuff in the bathtub and when I drink water!" *OK then!*

My three-year-old grandson was high stepping around the kitchen and shouting, "Right! Right! Right! Right!" So I asked him, "Are you marching?" He answered, "Noooo." So then I asked, "What are you doing then?" His answer: "I'm Righting!"

I said to my grandson, "You seem to be telling me "no" a lot these days and that's not a good thing. Why is that?" My grandson answered; "I don't know but don't worry about it!"

There was no school today for a state holiday and my grandson just informed me, "Grandma, I have to watch you." When I asked why, he said, "That's why I don't go to school today because I have to watch you."

My grandson said, "An ambulance is for when you are sick or mad or hurt." I told him, "No, an ambulance is just for when you get sick or hurt—not for when you get mad." He responded indignantly, "Not true! When you fall down you get mad!"

When the five-year-old I'm raising talked to his mother tonight about going to first grade next year, my addict daughter said, "Chevie, you need to stop growing so fast. You are just growing up too soon and I'm not ready for that, yet." He quickly answered her, "Mom, it's a part of life. You gotta just deal with it!" *I laughed so hard that I had tears rolling!*

We are forever grateful for our grandchildren's spontaneity, comedy and tenderness. The magnitude of what we do every day, along with the pain that may remain in our hearts, is lessened by the precious things they do and say. Their words and gestures give us unspeakable joy and will stay with us forever.

BLESSINGS EVERYWHERE

This is certainly an unexpected place we've landed, full of surprises and unforeseen blessings.

It isn't always easy and, of course, there are days we wonder what it would be like to just have "quiet" again. Then the kids go somewhere for the day and we find ourselves missing them. We miss their happy chatter in the house, even the messes to clean up. We miss everything about them and our life with them. We thought we were blessing these children by taking them in. But truly, these children have become blessings to us.

Sandee's Story

When precious little Cam came to us, he had intense anxiety and was very insecure. He had lost so much and wanting him to have a good life, we put all of our efforts and energy into raising him. We took him to play therapy and I always tried to ease his fears by reassuring him I would always be there for him.

Cam was just three years old when I planned to go on a much-needed two-day vacation with my sisters. I was leaving him at home with my husband, my grown daughter and my two younger daughters. I promised to wake him up before I left in the morning. As he awoke, he looked up at me with sleepy eyes and lovingly said with amazing insight for his age, "You are the best years of my life." It was all I could do not to cry and just stay home with him.

When Cam prayed, he always thanked God for giving him a home and a family. But every time Cam was thanking God for giving me to him, I was thanking God for the gift of this precious little boy in my life. I never dreamed when I prayed for strength in my journey it would come in the form of an innocent little boy. Cam has given me the power to endure this horrific journey. Only God knows if we will have a happy ending, but he has brought us this far and I will trust in Him always.

As a way of reaching out and giving back, I started a support group in our church for others who have shared my path. We pray together, encourage one another and even cry together. It has been a blessing to not be alone on this difficult journey and is my sincere hope that I can somehow be an inspiration to others.

BATTLE BUDDIES

Peer support is vital. In the army, Battle Buddies take care of each other on the battlefield, and off. They are not only assigned to each other for company but also for the reduction of suicide by watching each other's actions, noticing negative thoughts and intervening to save their buddy's life.

In our world where addiction is front and center, many of us have our own Battle Buddies who don't judge us but listen, support us and even offer coping skills.

These Battle Buddies come to us in a variety of ways. Sometimes it's an empathetic friend who is there for us with an open line and open arms. Some come to us by way of virtual interactive websites and some through face-to-face support groups. Whatever way support can be found is a hope chest and can offer camaraderie at a time when needed the most.

A grandmother on The Addicts Mom G2G (Grandparent to Grandparent) website, who was feeling alone and overwhelmed, apologized for ranting about her situation. Another grandmother responded, "Don't ever feel you have to apologize. Some days are harder than others. You're never alone as long as you have all of us. Hang in there and private message me if you want to talk one on one." Twenty-four more comments followed, either sharing related experiences or posting words of support and suggestions.

"I don't know what to do! My addict daughter was here to see her son, the one I'm raising. I asked her to leave because I could tell she was high and I didn't want her around the baby. She grabbed him from his play area and left. I'm so worried. I can't see straight. If I call, I don't think the police will do anything because she's the mother. Please, any advice?" Fifty-four grandparents responded with support, specifically about calling Child Protective Services and how to get emergency temporary custody.

Another grandparent shared, "I've had days when I've been so tired I didn't think I could do this anymore. I even thought of asking one of my other non-addict grown kids to raise my grandchild. But I felt too guilty and chickened out. Then, just as I was feeling so sorry for myself I was about to cry; my three grandchildren arrived home from school. They saw me sitting at the kitchen table and must have sensed my emotions. Suddenly, all three children hugged me and told me they were happy to be home. What could I say? That moment changed my attitude completely and made everything worthwhile."

No one can understand the gamut of emotions and magnitude of what we experience unless they have walked in our shoes. Having an ally to share feelings without shame and help problem-solve is validating and essential.

Our Battle Buddies, no matter what form they take, are lifesavers. We are so grateful for their support and truly need them to get us through this war.

Lynne's Story

When I first discovered The Addict's Mom website, I thought I was in a different place than most on the site. I was convinced I currently had my life handled. My son was thirteen years sober, working his program, helping others and living a beautiful life. My addict daughter was four years deceased and we were happy raising her son as our adopted son. I didn't realize it at the time, but I was not truly in touch with my feelings about her addiction or her death and how it affected me. Unconsciously—or maybe, consciously—I had pushed it aside, almost as if it never was. I thought it would be easier to go on without focusing on her or what had happened. But that was about to change.

Many women on the site were in great pain about their addict children and I thought I might be able to share my experience, which could help *them*. But I found just the opposite happened. Without their knowing, they helped *me*. When I exposed my feelings and comments were exchanged; relationships began to form. As a result, I discovered more about myself through them.

Even though addiction was not driving my life at that time, it was still part of my being and I was truly taken by surprise when I learned I was in more pain than I was willing to admit. It was through these women and their comments I gained insight into forgiveness and how to love the addict and not the disease. I was finally able to truly forgive and love my daughter, even in death. It has proved to be a valuable lesson regarding my way of thinking about my daughter, which, in turn, has been passed on to our son.

When the grandparent arm (G2G) of The Addict's Mom was formed, I was ready to humbly move on. I knew I was home. Being a grandparent raising a grandchild has its own unique challenges and being with these other grandparents in the same position opened up my world, as the focus was taken off the addict and put onto our grandchildren. We learn together, vent, resolve problems, question each other and share our sorrows, resentments and joys—all in the name of our grandchildren/children. This is where I found some life-altering messages, lifelong friends, but more importantly, where I found myself.

SURRENDER

A "moment of clarity" is often described as a sudden acceptance of some truth that, up until that moment, has been impossible to see. That term has been used pertaining to the alcoholic or addict who finally gets to that defining moment or lucidity that opens the door to their recovery. But everybody has them. As a parent of an addict, we too sometimes need a "moment of clarity" and some of us are lucky enough to receive one.

Laura's Story

Another support group meeting has left me with much more than I could possibly give. Again, I sat in awe as I listened to the stories. I found myself hanging onto the words of other family members as they freely shared their horror, their despair and their hope. As always, I tried to see if their experiences could shed some light on my own. I took careful note of the steps they were taking to see if my own should be altered. I looked for a glimmer of extra understanding I could use to strengthen and fortify my own resolve.

I found it.

It came as a memory that suddenly flashed into my mind from my own childhood.

Unexpected Heroes

I was four years old and I was helping my Dad load the car for a road trip. I grabbed the handle of a suitcase nearly as big as I was right behind his hand and lifted with all my strength. With patience and wisdom he slowed his steps and allowed me to "help" him. By lessening his hold just enough so I could feel some of the weight, I was forced to grip the handle as tightly as I could. He smiled as I grunted and strained and gave my very best effort towards moving that bag to its destination just a few feet away. I didn't want to admit I couldn't carry the load so I "gave" it back to him and then stepped back.

"Here, Daddy, you can do it now."

Then I watched as he quickly walked the remaining steps and effortlessly swung the bag up into the car.

My Dad knew there was no way I could possibly carry a bag that size by myself but rather than shoo me away, which would have certainly been much easier for him; he let me try. Really try.

The consequences of the choices my child has made are formidable. So much so, I am constantly struggling to wrap my mind around them as I try to think of possible solutions and scenarios that could somehow help her so the nightmare will go away.

I know there is truly nothing I can do. I know the efforts I may make to "lessen" her load are actually forcing her to carry it longer. Yet still, I am tightly gripping that handle. I am barely budging a load that I can't possibly carry. I am straining and pushing.

All the while, God is slowly walking beside me with great love and patience. Waiting for me to say the words.

"Here, Daddy. You can do it now."

Sometimes, understanding comes after long hard efforts of seeking it. Sometimes it surprises us when we weren't looking for it at all. And sometimes it was there all along.

JOY UNDEFEATED

Laura's Story

"**T**oday is my son's birthday. He is an addict. All I want to do is cry."

Reading these words written by another mother of an addicted child, sent me immediately back to a place where I was only few years ago, dealing with my own fear, uncertainty and grief. A time so crushing I could do nothing to escape it. I was consumed by worry and exhaustion from dealing with the impact on our family. The color of my whole world had changed. I tried the best I could to keep the chaos of emotions I felt under control so that I could attempt to function normally. But it was always there—just over the horizon or around the corner.

I remember being in the middle of a business meeting when thoughts of my daughter were suddenly overwhelming and sent me running to the restroom in tears. Another time, I was over-come during a church service and spent the rest of the hour crying in the car. I was so paralyzed by my grief over the child I had lost to the streets—the child I could not save, that I felt there was no escape. When I look back at that part of my past I can't even remember it in any other way but through that lens of grief.

Unexpected Heroes

Then, battle worn and drained; I was faced with another challenge when her baby arrived in the middle of the ongoing struggle. I knew we had to change our strategy and her success or failure battling addiction would no longer just directly affect her. Our new concern for the welfare of an innocent child changed our focus and forced us to take actions we would not have otherwise considered. As frightening new territory loomed ahead, the stress we felt was compounded. Added to it were feelings of resentment towards her choices and their impact upon us that caused even greater paralysis.

But finally, I came to an understanding—an epiphany. I realized it was one thing for my daughter to be ruining her own life but I was, at the same time, giving her permission to also ruin mine. I was allowing my joy to be stolen; almost as surely as leaving the doors and windows of a home knowingly unlocked in the presence of a thief. I decided I had to fight back and reclaim what I had lost.

The very first step I took, undoubtedly the most difficult, was to let my child go. In doing this I had to stop looking for her next misstep in hopes I could somehow do something in time to keep her from falling. I had told myself when the battle to save her began; it was better to be proactive than reactive. But this had given me permission to cross over the boundaries that protected my peace and enter into the war zone of her decisions. I realized it simply wasn't my battle to fight. Then I looked beyond the immediate situation and began to focus on the many blessings in my life I had neglected to appreciate by allowing them to be overshadowed. When I understood I was the only one who could do this, I felt a freedom return I had feared was permanently gone.

As parents of addicted children, we tell ourselves we are fighting to save them when often what we are really doing is hanging on tightly while they pull us down. The greatest gift we can give is to get out of the way so they can reach out on their own to the help waiting for them. By doing this, we are not only loving our children more than they can possibly understand, but also loving and being fully present for their children—our grandchildren—in the way they ultimately deserve.

ALWAYS HOPE

"When do you give up on your child?" This question was posed to a group of mothers of addicts and the answer was an immediate, resounding and unanimous, "Never!"

Hope's Story

Regardless of how long, difficult or daunting our journey along side our addicted child may be, sometimes, hope is all we have. "You never give up," one addict's mother said. "You just keep praying and hoping. You don't become engaged in their drug lives but let them know you are there for them, loving them from afar, waiting for them to get clean and sober."

As mothers, it is against our very nature to ever give up on our children, even when we are so damaged we don't "feel" it anymore. Some mothers have said that bitterness and resentment is hard to hold down and hope had indeed faded for them. "It's frightening to have hope," one mother admitted. "It scares me beyond my limits."

"Hope is fragile and I'm afraid to be disappointed again, like so many times before," another mom expressed.

But that could be fear talking. The fear your child will never get sober, the fear your child will never parent again and the worst fear of all—that your child will die. And so, we say we are afraid to hope, but it's really we're just afraid. The tendrils of hope are still woven deeply into our souls, sometimes only surfacing when the situation is too dire to rely on anything else.

Holding onto hope is only the tip of the iceberg, however. While we attempt to hold on, complicated issues such as enabling and codependency may interfere, and we must be even stronger in our dealings so that it is best for everyone involved. Hope without expectation is the attitude of some mothers. "You can step back, not have contact with your addict child and not give financial support," a mother shares. "But you always know, in the back of your mind, you can never give up."

Our lives are quite complex, keeping hope alive for our addict children and also parenting our addicted child's child and we must do things that sometimes seem unnatural like lovingly detaching. It's up to us to enforce distance and boundaries between the addicted child and the new life we, as grandparents/parents, are trying to establish for our grandchildren. We need to be focusing on building good lives for these children, not shaky foundations.

"Detaching is hard," a mother who has dealt with her child's addiction for seventeen years states. "But I've had to do it to keep my sanity and raise my grandchildren in a positive light."

Another mom who deals with her child from a distance said, "It was actually my disconnection from my son that brought me hope," she expressed. "I use a visualization my son, having nothing else to reach for, reached into his own heart, grasped onto an inner strength he didn't even know he had and rode it right to the top of a clean life."

The ability to "love our children from a distance" or detach, many times requires almost super human strength and yet it is necessary to protect our grandchildren, as well as give our children the greatest chance for recovery. "I walk in truth. My daughter's reality is harsh. She's reached the point of no return because she won't stop using, and her chronic health issues will take her life very soon," a mother tragically revealed. "Because she still uses, lies and steals, she cannot be around her children, whom I'm raising and so we must love her remotely. Hope allows us to carry the burden of reality and embrace the joy of raising her children."

For some of us, parenting our grandchildren, as difficult as it is, provides a diversion. Our day-to-day focus somehow has shifted to our grandchildren. Some of us have nestled nicely into our parenting roles and do not want our addict children involved, further complicating our already complicated relationships. The hopes and dreams we once had for our children, have now transferred, in part, to our grandchildren. Yet, for many, hope still lives silently inside of us.

"Even though they are not living the lives we'd hoped for them, no matter where they are, always let your children know they are loved," a mother cautions. "Your love could be what ends up saving them. Where there is love, there is hope."

In many ways, the most difficult thing to do is the most precious gift we could ever give. By truly letting go of them, we are giving our children another chance for life before it is too late. But letting go never means giving up. "Once I give up, my son will give up," was said by a stoic mother.

A grandmother, who never gave up on hope, shares her bittersweet story about the recovering addict parents and the grandchildren she took care of for almost two years. The bio parents, who have been clean for over a year, are reuniting with their children, whom she will now lose.

"My heart is breaking," she said. "I never thought this day would come. But I'm also happy their parents cared enough to get clean and continue to work on their sobriety." Holding back her tears, she added, "Friday will be difficult. I haven't even started packing because once I do; it becomes a reality. I will miss them dearly. Still, I look forward to being a grandma again—no more discipline, no more homework, no more rushing around to make sure everything was ready for school, sports, etc. I can now attend their activities, sit back and exclaim, "I'm Grandma!"

Hope never dies.

BY DAWN'S EARLY LIGHT

Laura's Story

When I walked into her room in the intensive care unit, I was immediately struck by how pretty she looked. Eyes closed, with her hair beautifully braided and draped gently across one shoulder. There was even a plumeria placed behind one ear. It's soft, fragrant petals brushed her cheek. Her petite fingers, although swollen, were perfectly polished and lay gracefully at her sides. My dear friend entered and practically fell into my arms. I held her and we cried together. When her sobbing subsided she asked me, "She looks good, doesn't she?"

I nodded.

"We braided her hair."

"She looks beautiful," I said.

We both knew this day was coming. After so many years of supporting each other, members of a club we never wished to join, she had said the words often, almost as if she was somehow preparing herself.

"You know she's going to die."

"I know."

But I had desperately hoped she was wrong. I had tried to hold onto the belief her daughter would somehow find her way back again because I was so afraid my own would follow her. But she wasn't wrong. When she called me the evening before to say they were removing life support the next day I promised I would come. I wanted to be there for her. I had to say "good- bye." I was awake before dawn that day. I couldn't sleep. Too many thoughts were screaming in my head; too many memories.

For years, the girls had walked the same path, sometimes together. My friend had watched carefully and often called me with updates on my own daughter's doings when she discovered details I didn't know. She cheered every time my daughter entered rehab and shared her regret that her own daughter would never go. She showered my daughter's sweet son with gifts upon his birth and cried with me when he was left in my care. When her own grandson was born she hung onto every word I shared about the steps I took to protect mine. Hers was only four months old when his mother left him forever.

As I lay there that morning contemplating the sadness of the steps I was about to take, it was a turning point for me. The impact of being so close to someone who was losing her child due to drugs had changed me. Cemented in my being, finally, was the truth that I could do nothing to stop my own child's addiction. But more than that, I had woken up to the reality and a new understanding of what was really important. I saw my beautiful daughter in a new light. For the first time in what seemed like forever, neither her actions, choices, nor even the pain I had felt colored my love for her.

There are too many stories of parents who have lost their precious children to addiction. I couldn't be more grateful that mine isn't one of them. My daughter is a hero. By definition a hero is someone who is a defeater, an example, someone who is greatly loved and admired. She is all of these. She has a long road ahead of her and she isn't perfect. But no hero ever is. And like every great hero, she is the epitome of hope. And that is her cherished gift to me.

A GRANDMOTHER'S HEART

Denise's Story

I've been lying here, as I sometimes do, thinking back to different times—younger days when life was good and safe and peaceful, when families were a priority and I could ride my bike with my brother to the penny candy store. Those were wonderful times…

Then I look at my grandchildren. They are so beautiful—one with eyes so large and the other with eyes so wise I can see forever in them both. God granted me the most precious privilege of being a grandparent. There is no greater love, no better peace, no bigger smile and no emotional warmth that can compare.

My granddaughter, my "heart princess puff" is a young child with a very old soul, whose hand warms my heart with just one touch. My grandson, my "soul bubba" brings a tear to my eye just thinking about the wonder of his wise mind and intensity of his being. Amazingly, they are a world in themselves.

I thank you, my glorious grandchildren, for all you are and are becoming. May you be blessed with the ability to dream and the desire to achieve. I wish for you the ability to blend kindness with tolerance, but my greatest hope for you is the love in your life is pure and unconditional.

Your journey has just begun. Keep your eyes wide open and try to see what others can't. Life is filled with surprises and many are good. If you don't keep watching for them, you'll miss half the fun. Expect to be thrilled once in a while—and you will be.

When you meet up with challenges, accept them head on for they'll leave you wiser, stronger and more capable than you were before. If you make a mistake, be grateful, and let those mistakes teach you so you won't make the same mistake twice. Resolve to use that lesson to help you reach your goals and to make your life better.

Always follow the rules—even the little ones. When rules are followed, life works. If you think you will ever get by with breaking the rules, you're only fooling yourself.

Be considerate and kind to those who love you and go out of your way to help people, especially the weak, the fearful and the innocent. Everyone carries a special sorrow and they need your compassion; especially when you may not realize it

Be truthful.

Don't yell. It never works and it can hurt both yourself and others.

Live in peace with nature. Appreciate God's gifts from the tiniest ant to the tallest tree.

Know what you want, keep your mind focused on it and be prepared to receive it.

Sometimes, you will have to be brave. Life isn't just about reaching peaks—it is about moving from one peak to the next. If you rest too long in between, you might be tempted to quit. Climb the mountain and enjoy the view and always move forward and never ever backward. Consider all the pathways ahead and decide carefully which to follow. Then along with belief in yourself, your faith and knowledge will help you take the right roads.

Shake off the things that weigh you down emotionally and spiritually. If a resentment, belief or attitude becomes heavy—let it go and lighten your load. Remember your choices will create your successes and your failures.

Don't forget to take breaks once in a while to rest. They'll give you a renewed commitment to your dreams and a cheerful, healthy perception of the things that matter the most.

Never worry about the things you may not have but always appreciate what you do. Treasure those closest to you. Move mountains for those who can't and love with the deepest part of your soul.

Most important, never give up on yourself. No matter what happens, the person who ends up a winner is the one who resolves to win. Give life everything you've got, and life will give it's best back to you.

I love you with all my heart and soul. You are a gift not only to me but also to the world.

MARCHING TO A
NEW DRUMMER

Acceptance of a new life centered on raising grandchildren is frequently a rude-awakening even for the most flexible of souls. The adjustment does not come easily, especially when other plans were in place and ready to be lived. Sometimes, messages come to us in the most unexpected and miraculous way, changing our perspectives and allowing joy to enter our souls.

Teresa's Story

I was sixty years old and I felt that my life was finally on the road to what I always dreamed it would be. I had moved up the corporate ladder and was happily making progress—even interviewing for a possible job in Peru. I loved my volunteer work teaching English to Hispanic immigrants. I was also back to focusing on my passion for art and was gleefully attending an acrylics painting class at the university all the while attending seminars and workshops on personal growth. My plan for paying off my mortgage and other debts was well under way, clearing the path to finally being able to change location and begin the next chapter of my life. I was so happy it was all coming together. I was ready to fully embrace my golden years...and then the call came.

"I didn't know if I should call you or not," said this person, whose voice was vaguely familiar. "I'm calling because I love her and am worried she is going to die."

"What? Who is this and what is going on?" I asked.

"It's Liz's friend, Amy," the concerned voice answered. "You need to do something to help Liz. She is using heroin every day all day and she's not taking care of her kids."

I hung up the phone. Before I could digest what I just heard or even react, a second call came in. Liz and her boyfriend were arrested in a motel room and charged with drug use and endangering children. Their three children were with them. I was horrified but grateful to be able to quickly get there and take the children. That's when Children's Services and I began our long-term relationship. I, and other family members, were fingerprinted, investigated and interviewed before being granted temporary guardianship.

My life, as I thought it would be, began to unravel right before my eyes.

My beloved daughter was taken to jail. Since it was her first offense, she was given probation and ordered to attend Intensive Outpatient (IOP) classes. That didn't work and her addiction returned with a vengeance. I continued to care for her children but I still held onto hope she would get better and become the kind of mother her children needed. Failing IOP, she went to her first residential detox center but was discharged after a week because her insurance wouldn't cover more time.

Not knowing what else to do, I would hold her children in front of her like they were prizes she could win, if she became sober. It made perfect sense to me. What mother wouldn't be willing to do whatever was necessary to get her children back? If only, that could have worked.

She reluctantly went to a rehab facility in another city but returned after a month. She tried several more rehabs—even our family intervened—but her stays were always temporary and unsuccessful.

My hope was she would become a responsible woman and mother, but she was back to her destructive behavior. I was robbed of all my jewelry, including sentimental pieces; medicines and even the kids' piggy banks were emptied. How could she? I was so angry with my daughter and the situation. I resented her and hated she had destroyed my future. The life I was looking forward to was never going to happen. Devastated, I realized I'd never be the same.

The children stayed with me while Children's Services pushed me to either become their legal guardian or put the children into foster care. I became their legal guardian. With three children under eight years old, my life had been transformed into a never-ending cycle of work, dinner, baths, homework, school events, sports teams and finally, bedtime. Too often, my own slumber was the highlight of my day.

I used to shudder when friends and acquaintances would say, "I really respect you and all you do for those kids. I don't know if I could do it!" My kneejerk reply always was, "Oh, I just do what I need to because I love the children. I am blessed to be able to do this." I thought if I said it often enough, I would eventually believe it. They had no idea what I was feeling or going through.

As guardian of my grandchildren, my days were a mixed bag ranging from okay to just awful. Every once in a while, there was a really good day and that helped me to keep going. I hoped to have my life back again someday—that this was only temporary. But every time I got my hopes up, something happened and I was disappointed.

My daughter and her husband had been in residential rehab for almost three months, but as soon as they received their tax refund check, they left. I was sure they took the money and went on a shopping spree, enjoyed eating out and living a nice little—albeit temporary—life. I felt my resentment flare up. She was free to go and do whatever she wanted, but I was stuck at home caring for her children with my life on hold. She managed to check in with the children every couple days just to alleviate her guilt. I believe after she hung up, she crossed her "mom duties task" off her list and went back to her "real life." I'd often ask myself, "Why don't I have a real life?"

I was so embittered by what her addiction had done to my life. I completely gave up my dream; and became so consumed with regret and resentment, I could hardly see straight. I tried to take care of the children as best I could, but I'm sure they sensed my misery. I didn't think I could take one more day living like this when, quite by accident, I stumbled onto these words by Father Alfred D'Souza:

> *For a long time it had seemed to me that life was about to begin—real life. But there was always some obstacle in the way, something to be got through. First, some unfinished business, time still to be served, a debt to be paid—then life would begin. At last it dawned on me that these obstacles were my life.*

The moment I read those words, a calm came over me as the meaning of the words sunk in. This was exactly what I needed to hear. I felt like it was written just for me. Finally, I understood that regardless of how I felt, this *was* my life. Suddenly I realized no one forced me to choose it. I chose it myself. One could argue I didn't have a choice to step in and help my grandchildren—but I did. I could have chosen foster care for them or even possibly adoption but I didn't feel that was best. I *chose* what I felt was best. No one was holding a gun to my head. For whatever reason, through my understanding of this, God changed my life's direction and I finally got it; somehow I understood and I was immediately changed.

This epiphany didn't make my days any easier, but it made them more meaningful. Miraculously, the resentment I felt towards my daughter seemed to disappear. I still didn't like what she did to herself and to our family, but I felt love for her in spite of it and no longer was waiting for her to "get better." I simply prayed she would. But it was her life and up to her.

My life is now mom/grandma to three children. Before, I was just going through the motions, but these children deserve the best I have to give. Now, I am doing it with laughter, smiles and devoted love. My role in life is to raise these children to become loving, happy and successful adults. As they say: "It's a tough job but someone has to do it." Thankfully, I can now honestly say that I've become the best person for that job.

GETTING OUR LIVES BACK

Who knows what tomorrow will bring? For today, we are in a different place—a place we never imagined existed. We must make the best of this new frontier. We must borrow from the past and rebuild for the present and future. We must relish the goodness of these times and set aside the bad. Life has a way of coming around again. Who knows what tomorrow may bring...

Julie's Story

While visiting my husband, who works out of town most of the time, Kyler and I were involved in an accident with a drunk driver, which resulted in the death of an eighteen-year-old passenger in the other car. This affected Kyler more profoundly than most other children, I think. His first response was to pray for the people in the other car. His second response was almost like Post Traumatic Stress Disorder in that he feared for me to travel after that. He really didn't want me traveling without him because he feared something might happen and he wouldn't be there to take care of me. He was constantly hugging me, kissing me and saying, "I love you, Mom."

Unexpected Heroes

Years have gone by and I look at him now at age fourteen. And although there are those "teenage moments," he is all in all a really good kid. His cell phone seems to run down more quickly than mine because of all of the incoming text messages. He runs me ragged and I feel like I'm a taxi service. He's awkward at times and incredibly funny. Scraggly little teenage mustache and hairy legs—where did the time go? But he still hugs me and kisses me and says, "I love you, Mom."

The teenage girls are just crazy about him. He still likes to do family trips and adventures. He is all boy. He's my last one.

In four more years, my nest will be empty after thirty-five years of raising children. It is hard for me to grasp that concept. No more children living at home. I will miss him terribly. I'm hoping at some point to be a grandma again—but this time to be a real grandma. It sounds like a job I might just love.

ACCEPTING THE NEW NORMAL

Laura's Story

I was tired. My four-year-old grandson, of whom I was legal guardian, woke up hacking in the throws of an asthma attack. I couldn't help groaning as I surfaced from the depths of sleep when I first heard him. I didn't want to look at the time. Five o'clock and the morning scramble would come around soon enough and I would rather not know if I only had an hour left to sleep. But he kept coughing and so I waited for him to wake up with a familiar call.

Fitfully, I tossed and turned for what seemed like forever, teetering on waves of sleep only to be snapped back to alertness by the sounds of the next cough through the monitor. I decided I'd look at the time and just get up if it was close to the alarm. That way I could get some coffee and continue to watch him. But it was only three o'clock and the intensity of his coughing steadily increased. Clearly he was going to need a breathing treatment if either of us was going to get any sleep.

It became evident our grandson had asthma when he was still a baby. Frantic trips to the doctor and emergency room were made even more frightening due to the knowledge my husband had lost his own brother as a toddler to asthma. These concerns had compounded our ongoing stress due to our daughter's struggles with addiction. Without a choice, our focus quickly became her child and almost thirty years after the birth of our first child; we signed papers that stated we were willingly bearing the full responsibility of being parents, yet again.

I remember having so many people asking me the same question, "So how does it feel to be a grandparent?" The truth was I had absolutely no idea. In fact, I honestly wished I did know. What I felt for my grandson was essentially what I felt for each of my own children. But the difference thirty years made was impossible to ignore.

It was flattering to occasionally be mistaken for our grandson's parents, but I always wondered what the well-meaning observer really thought. Undeniably the biggest impact was simply the sheer, sometimes overwhelming work of raising another child. I often asked myself how in the world I did it before, raising three children, even in my twenties. But now, at a time in my life when I should have been able to kick back and relax, when I should have finally earned some time for myself—it was impossible to even read a book without interruption. Grateful for good health, I knew the odds were much higher than when my first child was small, and this could easily change.

Occasionally, I had struggled with my sudden new role. Along with parenting a toddler, I was at the same time also executor of my parent's estate and custodial guardian of my mother's care in the late stages of Alzheimer's Disease. And then there was my immediate family. My "baby," my son was still living at home, going to college and dealing with his own fears and anxieties as he faced his future in the wake of the stress we had endured as a family. No one was immune from its impact. I wondered if my life would ever settle down and even vaguely resemble what I once considered to be "normal" again, and then what in the world would that even look like? I finally realized, I had to stop questioning, accept and embrace what was, if I had any hope of retrieving the peace and joy in my life that I felt had been lost. And so that's what I did.

I could hear my grandson's gentle wheezing begin to lessen after the treatment he barely seemed to notice and waited for the coughing to subside before trying to go back to sleep. To pass the time, I let my mind wander and in my head, played back pieces of one of my favorite Broadway musicals. I remembered fondly how my husband had decided it was the perfect idea to purchase tickets and see that show a few years ago right in the middle of the chaos that had become our life. He was right. It was wonderful, even better than I had imagined.

Glancing at the time, I knew I'd be fighting back yawns as I tried to read stories and teach my first graders math the next day. My grandson was oblivious to my predawn sleep interruption. Chocolate curls framed his face and so-long-it's-not-fair black eyelashes brushed against his cheeks while he slept. In the morning, I knew he wouldn't even remember I came into his room.

I didn't underestimate for a moment the importance of my place in his life. I had no idea what it was like to be a grandmother yet, but that really didn't matter. I was no more a traditional grandparent than he was a traditional grandchild and in a strange way, that thought was somehow appealing to me. Bonded by unexpected circumstances beyond anyone's control, he had brought unbelievable joy and peace into our lives. The wounds from the past were slowly healing and we were finding a new "normal."

Gradually, my perception of what "should be" was changing and I slipped less often into periods of resentment. I grew confident in my understanding, wisdom and acceptance of things I simply could not change. Most of all, in spite of everything, because of this child—because I knew him, I had been changed... for good.

EPILOGUE

Addiction is a poorly understood monster, especially by those fortunate enough to have avoided its devastating impact. We, who have suffered its consequences, shared our stories to provide understanding, strength and hope to both the afflicted and inexperienced.

We are raising our children's children because of this illness, and hope those who share our circumstances now know they are far from alone. For those who are looking in, we hope you have gained an understanding of how deeply addiction impacts the lives of those who never dreamed it would happen to them. We have been compelled to come to terms with this fiend by seeking out as much information as possible, not just because we have addicted children whom we love, but because we are currently raising children of addicts—our grandchildren—and we must do our very best for them.

Without treatment or commitment to recovery, addiction is progressive and often results in disability or too frequently, premature death. When such a tragedy occurs, it is usually the family members who must step in to pick up the pieces of the victims' shattered lives as well as endure the consequences and collateral damage that loving a drug addict causes.

Unexpected Heroes

The ongoing debate as to the cause of drug addiction matters very little when the life of a child is at stake. As mothers, we love our children, offer them as many options as we can for treatment and struggle with how much or how little support should be offered. Ultimately the motivation for recovery has to come from the addict.

In the meantime, scores of families are locked in a literal fight for the lives of their children and their children's children as the war on drugs rages all around us.

God grant me the serenity
To accept the things I cannot change,
Courage to change the things I can,
And the wisdom to know the difference.

—*THE SERENITY PRAYER*

VII

SURVIVAL GUIDE

"Heroism is endurance for one moment more."

—*George Kennan*

PREPARE FOR DEFENSE

Many grandparents lack information about addiction and the range of support services, resources, programs, financial benefits, laws and policies available to help successfully fulfill our parenting role. The following resources and information can help.

Addiction

Two hundred thousand deaths were due to drug and alcohol abuse in 2010, according to the *United Nations Report*, and that number is even higher today with heroin-related overdose deaths almost quadrupling between 2002 and 2013.

The initial decision to take drugs is usually voluntary with a multitude of reasons, but very quickly addiction can take over. Choice no longer becomes a viable option as evidenced by imaging studies from addicted brains. These images show actual physical changes in areas critical for judgment, decision-making, learning, memory and behavior control.

The Substance Abuse and Mental Health Services Administration's *2013 National Survey on Drug Use and Health* reported that an estimated 24.6 million Americans aged twelve or older were illicit drug users. The National Institute on Drug Abuse reported that out of an estimated 23.1 million Americans needing treatment for a problem related to drugs or alcohol, only about 2.5 million people (one percent) received treatment at a specialty facility. On average, between twenty-five and fifty percent of drug users who receive treatment return to using drugs within just two years of receiving rehabilitation. Addicts who can completely abstain from all drug use for five years still have a fifteen-percent chance of relapse. Even so, it's sometimes two steps back and one step forward before acceptance and success can come for the struggling addict.

Adoption

In order to adopt a child, the birth parents' rights must be terminated. An adoption application needs to be filed with the probate court along with an agreement of adoption. The Department of Social Services will investigate and determine whether the applicant would be a good adoptive parent. If the child is twelve years or older, he or she must also agree to be adopted. The fees vary greatly according to individual state department, lawyer, home study, finger print scan and heath physical fees. Adoption fees can be steep and can often range anywhere from five to fifteen thousand dollars. However, there is a one-time Federal Adoption Credit (see below under National Assistance), which pays for most of the adoption expenses, as long as certain requirements are met.

Books for Adults

Bailey, Laura Montane, LMFT. *Courageous Love: Instructions for Creating Healing Circles for Children of Trauma.* Indiana: iUniverse

LLC, 2013. This book explores the impact of trauma on the grandchild and offers Healing Circles as a method to help the children experience growth and foster a sense of belonging.

Beattie, Melody. *Codependent No More: How To Stop Controlling Others And Start Caring For Yourself.* Minnesota: Hazelden, 1992. The healing touchstone of millions, this book offers the key to understanding codependency and unlocking its stultifying hold on life.

DeToledo, Sylvie and Deborah Edler Brown. *Grandparents As Parents-2nd Edition: A Survival Guide for Raising a Second Family.* New York: Guilford Press, 2013. This book by offers effective strategies to cope with the stresses of raising a family for the second time.

Doucette, Deborah and Dr. Jeffrey LaCure. *Raising Our Children's Children: Room In The Heart-2nd Edition.* Maryland: Taylor Trade Publishing, 2014. Filled with true stories from people who have raised their children's children, and including advice from Dr. Jeffrey R. LaCure, Family and Adoption Therapist, throughout; this family-focused book looks at this fairly common relationship from all sides, offers advice, information, help and healing.

Gassel, Lynne R. *Fifth Child: The Turbulent Path That Led to Parenting Our Child's Child.* California: LRSG House, 2013. A compelling story of a mother's arduous journey through her daughter's addiction, its devastating consequences and a family's path to recovery; a result of raising Brady, her fifth child.

Moe, Jerry, MA. *Understanding Addiction and Recovery Through a Child's Eyes: Hope, Help, and Healing for Families.* Florida: Health Communications, Inc. 2007. This insightful book is about children, who have reclaimed their self-worth in spite of living in the shadow of addiction.

Sheff, David. *Clean: Overcoming Addiction And Ending America's Greatest Tragedy.* New York: Houghton Mifflin Harcourt, 2013. This is a myth-shattering look at drug abuse and treatment by the best-selling author of *Beautiful Boy.*

Swenson, Sandra. *The Joey Song.* Nevada: Central Recovery Press, 2014. This is a poignant story orchestrating a mother's lessons of love and loss, while surviving her son's addiction. The author's words are pearls.

Williams, Elaine K. *The Sacred Work of Grandparents Raising Their Grandchildren.* Indiana: Balboa Press, 2011. This book contains invaluable insights addressing unique issues faced by grandparents raising grandchildren.

Wright, Karen Best. *I Love You From The Edges: Lessons From Raising Grandchildren.* Indiana: Author House, 2014. The author raised her grandchildren for seven years (not due to addiction) and had to give them back. Her story is about lessons, relationships and the importance of getting and staying healthy.

Books for Children

Hastings, Jill M. and Marion H. Typpo. *An Elephant In the Living Room.* Minnesota: Hazelden, 1994. This is an illustrated story to help young children understand and cope with alcoholism or drug addiction in the family.

Holmes, Margaret M. and Sasha J. Mudlaff. *A Terrible Thing Happened*. Maryland: Magination Press, 2000. The character in the book saw a terrible thing happen. He felt very afraid until he met someone who helped him talk about it and will help children express feelings.

Spelman, Cornelia Maude. *(Way I Feel Books)*: *When I Miss You, When I Feel Scared, When I Feel Sad, When I Feel Angry, When I Feel Worried*. Illinois: Albert Whitman & Company, 2004. Young children in a variety of stressful situations have to deal with many feelings. These books address those different situations, feelings and ways to cope.

Straus, Susan Farber. *Healing Days: A Guide for Kids Who Have Experienced Trauma*. Maryland: Magination Press, 2013. This is a sensitive story designed to be read by a parent to a child who has experienced trauma.

Thomas, Pat. *I Miss You: A First Look at Death*. Great Britain: Hodder Wayland, 2001. This book helps young children see death as a natural complement to life and encourages kids to be in touch with and express feelings, especially grief.

Boundaries

Trust Your Gut: A mother of an addict once said, "My gut has a one hundred percent perfect record. Every time it told me something wasn't right, it wasn't. Listen to your gut. It never lies."

Being the Good Guy: Do not fear being disliked because of certain decisions needed to be made. Allowing an addicted child in the house with grandchildren present and causing emotional upheaval is not healthy for them or for us. We must ask ourselves if our decision is safe for our home and family. The family must be protected.

Enabling: If it doesn't have your name on it, don't open it. We are not helping our addict by paying their bills or parking tickets. The same goes for filling their gas tanks or giving them money for incidentals. We think we are helping but we are not. What we are helping to do is fuel their addiction. By paying their bills, etc., we are freeing up their own money to purchase substances that threaten their safety and life. A young man, in recovery, once said the next time your loved one asks for five dollars and you give in, stating clearly, "this is the last time"—it might very well be the last time.

Follow-Through: Stick to your guns and your answer. If you give into the pleading, your word and your authority will be meaningless. If conditions or threats are made, follow through with consequences. Yes is yes and no is no. Once you give in and go back on what you've said, you lose to addiction.

Know Your Limits: Balance in life is important. No one person is responsible for solving the problems or meeting the needs of everyone around them. No one person is responsible for making sure the world runs efficiently. Nothing we do will force another person to comply with our wishes, abide by our rules or agree with everything we say. However, we can and must set healthy boundaries for ourselves, and our homes. We must take care of ourselves first before we can have the strength to stand up to the stress of dealing with an addicted child.

Okay to Disconnect: In this age of technology, many of us are "signed in" all the time. It's almost uncomfortable to disconnect. We seem to feel a responsibility to our virtual friends, their problems and their successes, which takes us away from living in the real world.

Statements of Regret: In the heat of an argument, don't allow your emotions make you do or say something you will live to regret. Tomorrow is never promised and your last words should never be said in anger. The sad truth is, when dealing with addicts, those may be the last words you say to them. The argument will give them the excuse they need to go out and use and their "one last time" might actually be the last time.

Documentation/Documents

Documentation is necessary. From the time the grandparent takes over caring for the child, a log, calendar or diary should be kept with dates and details of encounters, no-shows, behavior, etc. This can be beneficial when applying for guardianship, filing for adoption or to support a case with Social Services or in a court of law.

Documents: Certain documents are necessary to have in the grandparent's possession:

- Birth certificate (child and grandchild)
- Death certificate (if your grandchild's parent is deceased).
- Marriage records or divorce decrees (for their parents, if applicable).

- Social Security cards (or at least the numbers) for the children.
- Medical and dental records, psychological and/or neuro-psychological evaluations.
- Immunization Records
- Power of Attorney, custody, guardianship, adoption or other legal papers.
- Consent forms signed by the parents for medical care and education, if the grandparent does not have guardianship.
- School papers such as report cards, evaluations, registration, etc.
- Proof of your grandchild's income and assets (child support payments, trusts, etc.).

Drugs

In addition to the more commonly known abused drugs such as alcohol, marijuana, heroin, methamphetamines, cocaine, inhalants, ecstasy, prescription drugs and hallucinogens, etc., an abundance of derivatives, synthetic and "designer" drugs have emerged. These drugs are deemed legal because production is so fast with so many formulations on the market, the U.S. Drug Enforcement Administration (DEA) cannot get to them quickly enough to ban. These recreational drugs are putting unsuspecting users at risk not only for addiction but also severe side effects, physical harm and even death.

Guardianship

Emergency Custody or in some states is called Immediate Temporary Custody, is necessary if you suspect there is a grave and immediate threat to the child from a parent. This type of guardianship is always temporary. Either you will need to apply for a permanent custody change or, per to your state or municipality; the court will hold a second custody hearing.

Legal Guardianship has different rules for every state, county and municipality, dictating which court takes care of family law issues, requirements, fee schedules and its unique name for guardianship. An application can usually be made directly to the court or privately through an attorney. In either case, you will need to provide documentation about why you are requesting guardianship. The process is also easier if you can get the bio parent or parents to consent to guardianship. A hearing is arranged before a judge to award guardianship.

Before the hearing, a social worker from the Department of Children and Families (DCF) or Department of Social Services (DSS) will speak with the grandparent or relative and may conduct a home visit to make sure the applicant is able to provide safe and stable care of the child. If awarded, temporary custody remains in effect until the child turns eighteen years of age. The biological parent can always petition the court to regain custody of their child. These terms may also vary according to state.

Standby Guardianship is custody of a child that can be obtained without going to court. According to the American Association of Retired Persons (AARP), standby guardianship is created by having the parents sign a document available from the probate court stating that they are consenting to have the grandparent or relative take guardianship of their child. This can go into effect when a triggering event occurs such as if the parents are temporarily unable to care for a child due to physical or mental disability, residence in a drug or alcohol rehabilitation program, going to jail for a period of less than one year or other absence from home. Standby guardianship lasts up to one year.

Termination of Parental Rights is a final court order that completely severs the legal relationship between the parents and the child. According to AARP, the court may terminate parental rights if one or more of the following conditions can be proven:

- The parents have consented to the termination;
- The child has been abandoned by the parents;
- The parents and child have no ongoing relationship;
- The child was found to be neglected, was in the care of DCF for at least fifteen months, and the parents have failed to improve enough to parent safely;
- The child is under age seven years, and is neglected, and the parental rights to another child were previously terminated and the parents have not been rehabilitated;
- The child has suffered abuse because of the parents' actions or failure to act;
- The parent seriously injured or attempted to seriously injure another of his/her children; or
- The parent was convicted in court of a sexual assault that resulted in the child's conception.

If only one parent's rights are terminated, the other parent will become the child's sole parent and legal guardian. If both parents' rights are terminated, a grandparent, relative, or someone else will be appointed as guardian. A person applying as the child's guardian may be appointed at the same time that parental rights be terminated. To be appointed as the guardian, the probate court will ask for an investigation to determine the physical, mental, social, and financial conditions of the parents and the grandparents or relatives applying for guardianship. If the court grants guardianship, it will issue a written decree removing the parents as guardians and appointing the applicant as guardian in their place. It may also grant visitation rights to one or both parents or to other family members. Guardianship remains in effect until one or both parents apply to have their guardianship rights reinstated, until the guardian resigns or is removed, or until the child turns eighteen.

In most cases where a grandparent is appointed as guardian, there are usually no state or court fees. However, if privately applying for legal guardianship, which many grandparents do, there will be lawyer and other incidental fees.

National Assistance

Child and Dependent Care Credit can help families who pay for childcare so they are able to work or look for work. Caregivers do not need legal guardianship but the child must be defined as the caregiver's dependent.

Child Tax Credit offers a credit of up to one thousand dollars per child. The maximum income allowable is higher than other credits so more families may be eligible. Caregivers do not need legal guardianship but the child must be defined as the caregiver's dependent.

Earned Income Tax Credit is available for grandparents raising grandchildren. It has certain income requirements depending on the number of children being raised but the grandparent does not have to have legal guardianship. The child must be a relative, have lived with the grandparent for more than half of the filing year and be under nineteen years of age, a full-time student under the age of twenty-four or totally disabled.

Federal Adoption Credit is a one-time credit that can be taken off your taxes up to a maximum amount. The considerable amount of credit awarded is according to income. Expenditures for adoption plus expenses for guardianship are reimbursed as a tax credit.
www.Nacac.org

Health Insurance through the Affordable Care Act offers a streamlined enrollment to get health care for those who are eligible. An affordable pediatric health insurance for children, which includes vision, is available. Pediatric dentistry is additional but reasonably priced. If you are on Medicare and need insurance for your grandchild, this is a good option.

Medicaid is in all states but might go under a different name such as Medi-Cal, California's program.
www.medicaid.gov

Supplemental Nutrition Assistance Program (SNAP) is the new name for the Federal Food Stamp Program for individuals and low-income families. Although SNAP is the national name, your state may use a different name. Financial assistance varies from state to state.

Social Security Benefits are multigenerational across our nation. In addition to Retirement and Disability benefits, Survivor's Benefits are available if the child's parent is deceased, even if the grandparent is raising the child. It is based on the parent's earnings. If the child is adopted, the benefits can be distributed according the grandparent's earnings if it was more than what the parent earned. Contact Social Security Administration:

1-800-772-1213

www.socialsecurity.gov

Supplemental Security Income (SSI) program pays benefits to disabled adults and children who have limited income and resources. SSI benefits are also payable to people sixty-five and older without disabilities that meet the financial limits. Social Security Administration office:

1-800-772-1213

www.socialsecurity.gov

WIC Food Program is a supplemental nutrition for women, infants and children (until age five years). Federal grants are given to each state for supplemental foods, nutrition education and health care referrals.

www.fns.usda.gov/wic/women-infants-and- children-wic

State Assistance

Benefits available vary state-by-state and have very specific requirements. The financial assistance is not enough to support a golden age family but can be helpful as a supplement. The most comprehensive website is American Association of Retired Persons (AARP). Facts, data and financial assistance information are listed concerning grandparents raising grandchildren. On the website see GrandFacts State Fact Sheets to access your state.

www.aarp.org/relationships/friendsfamily/grandfacts-sheets/

Housing for grandparents raising grandchildren is available in a few cities such as Boston, MA, Bronx, New York, Baton Rouge, Louisiana and soon in Newark, NJ. For more information, go to:

www.gu.org

Non-Needy Stipends or **Assistance for Relatives Raising Relatives** is available in some states and are not based according to income.

Temporary Assistance to Need Families (TANF) is set aside by the Federal government for every working family under a certain income level. There is also a "Child-Only" version, where income is not a requirement and does not rely on the income status of the caregiver. The only stipulation is that temporary or permanent custody through juvenile court, children services or a foster care agency be in place.

Websites/Blogs/Support

Al-Anon/Alateen/Alatot offers hope to families and friends of addicts/alcoholics via Twelve-Step Meetings. Alateen is for teens and Alatot for young children.

www.al-anon.com

American Association of Retired Persons (AARP) offers information and support for grand families.

www.aarp.org>relationships>grandaprenting

Changing Lives Foundation is an informative website with a focus on recovery for friends and family of addicts/alcoholics.

www.ChangingLivesFoundation.org

www.drug-addiction-help-now.org/blog/

Cathy Taughinbaugh helps parents find peace through her blog, personal coaching and her support groups.

www.cathytaughinbaugh.com

Co-Dependents Anonymous (CoDA) offers support group meetings for recovery from codependence.

www.locator.coda.org

Grandparents.com Community is a website with current information and a place for grandparents to post.

www.community.grandparents.com

Elaine Nicholas, Compassion Fatigue Educator

www.creatingahaven.com

Families In the Fire is a non-profit organization that offers support to Hawaii's families whose loved ones are caught in the snare of methamphetamine addiction.

www.familiesinthefire.com

Generations United is an informational website for Grand Families.

www.gu.org/grandfamilies

Grandparents As Parents (GAP) offer group support via small group meetings specifically in California.

818-264-0880

info@grandparentsasparents.org

GrandparentsRaisingGrandchildren is a Blog by Karen Best Wright offering up-to-date and pertinent information.

www.grandparentingblog.com.

Kids Health Website offers information dealing with life stresses, emotions, drugs and coping with death.
www.kidshealth.org

National Alliance On Mental Illness (NAMI) offers information and support concerning mental illness.
www.nami.org

Relatives Raising Children (RRC) is a closed site for relatives raising grandchildren not necessarily due to addiction. To request membership/information:
www.raisinggrandchildren@earthlink.net

The Addict's Mom is an interactive "Closed Group" support website for mothers and other relatives of addicts to share without shame.
www.facebook.com/groups/theaddictsmom/

The Addict's Mom G2G (Grandparent to Grandparent) is an interactive "Closed Group" support website specifically for grandparents raising grandchildren.
www.facebook.com/groups/154033158118579/

The Sober World Magazine is an online and tangible publication offering compelling informative articles concerning every aspect of addiction.
www.thesoberworld.com